THE ART
OF
SELF-PROMOTION

"A helpful tool in developing your best career manager — you."

Kristy Weathers, Professional Development Partner, Sutherland

"This book leverages all of Stone's considerable executive coaching experience and will be enlightening and helpful to CEOs of growing businesses as well as to the people they lead."

Andy Berg, CFP®, CEO, Homrich Berg

"Telling your story effectively is critical. This book does a masterful job of teaching you how to do that confidently and authentically to advance your career."

Amena Ali, SVP & General Manager, WeatherBug Home

"This book provides practical insights about effective self-promotion that students and early career professionals can readily understand and immediately apply in the workplace."

La Tondra Murray, Ph.D., Director, Pratt Professional Masters Programs, Duke University

"Even those of us who have risen to a level of professional success can be reminded of our need for efficient and effective self-promotion."

Lori Reese Patton, Chief Learning Officer & Special Counsel, Womble, Carlyle, Sandridge & Rice, LLP

"In today's highly competitive environment, it is essential for C-level executives to be role models for extolling the benefits of their company's products or services. This book tells you and your team how!"

Garrett R. D'Alessandro, Chief Executive Officer, City National Rochdale Investments

"Debby's writing is so approachable – This book is the perfect how-to guide for anyone who wants to learn to master the art of self-promotion."

Lisa Burke, MD

"Self-promotion is truly an art, and Stone's insight, guidance, and tools are invaluable to all – from students to managers to C-suite executives to entrepreneurs. Career advisors and our clients should pick up this book and keep it handy at all stages of career growth, including networking opportunities, interviews, annual reviews, and media interviews."

Emily Kapit, MS, MRW, ACRW, CPRW,
Triple Certified Resume Writer and Lead Career Strategist, ReFresh Your Step Career Development & Advisory

TELL YOUR STORY, TRANSFORM YOUR CAREER

Debby Stone, JD, CPCC, PCC

Foreword by Dr. Alan Zimmerman

The Art of Self-Promotion: Tell Your Story, Transform Your Career

Published by:
Novateur Publishing – Debby Stone
1629 Monroe Drive NE
Atlanta, GA 30324
404-975-3000
www.artofselfpromotionbook.com

Printed in the United States of America by: BookLogix
1264 Old Alpharetta Road
Alpharetta, GA 30005
470-239-8547

Author: Debby Stone, JD, CPCC, PCC
Cover Design: Chris Gorton
Internal Design: Steven Sharp
Project Management: Bonnie Daneker, Write Advisors, LLC

ISBN: 978-0-9967458-0-2
First Printing: October 2015

While the examples and stories in this book are based upon real client situations, names and identifying characteristics of the persons involved have been changed to respect the confidentiality of the coaching relationship and the identities of the individuals.

Library of Congress Control Number: 2015913879
Stone, Debby
The art of self-promotion: tell your story, transform your career / Debby Stone
1. Career 2. Self-promotion 3. Success 4. Leadership
5. Business Communication

To my husband and partner in life, Dan Sheedy.

Table of Contents

Foreword

by Dr. Alan Zimmerman

The elusive missing ingredient in career success… people have been looking for that for years.

As a youngster, I thought the secret was IQ. If a person was lucky enough to be born with a lot of it, I was certain that person would be a huge success at whatever career he or she chose.

Later I learned that there's little or no correlation between IQ and career success. Haven't you ever met someone who's too smart for their own good?

As a student working on my various degrees, I thought the secret was grades. Even though I might not be the smartest person at the university, I reasoned that no one could outwork me. No one could study longer or harder than me. That proved to be true, and I did graduate at the top of all my classes with the highest academic honors.

However, the research shows that many successful leaders graduated in the bottom half of their classes.

Obviously, neither one of those two items was the missing or so-called "secret ingredient" in career success.

I then embarked on a 30-year research project to discover the "secret." My conclusion came down to a simple formula, that Purpose + Passion + Process = Payoff. A person must have all three elements to ensure the payoffs — life and career success — he desires.

First of all, Purpose. If a person doesn't stand for something, he will fall for anything. It's purpose that gives meaning to a person's life and career. And purpose can be discovered and/or clarified, if need be.

Second, Passion. Passion is the fuel that keeps a person going in good times and bad. It is a combination of attitude, persistence and character, all of which can be built and maintained, if a person knows and uses the right skills.

Third, Process. Some people have an admirable purpose and a burning passion, but their results are dismal. They didn't have much to show for all their good intentions and hard work. They desperately need some personal and professional processes to bring it all together.

I am still convinced that my formula of Purpose + Passion + Process = Payoff is the way to incredible success, and it will work for anyone in any career or any place in life.

However, I now know there is one more critical ingredient in the formula for success, and Debby Stone has eloquently revealed that all-important ingredient in this ever-so-valuable volume.

After all, a person could have a clear purpose, plenty of passion and some effective processes, and still not get his career off the ground, because he is lacking one more crucial thing: the ability to self-promote.

> However, I now know there is one more critical ingredient in the formula for success, and Debby Stone has eloquently revealed that all-important ingredient.
> *—Dr. Alan Zimmerman*

Quite sadly, most everyone needs a great deal more of this self-promotion skill. And until now, there have been very few resources available to teach a person how to do it well.

The result has been that people tend to go to one extreme or another when it comes to self-promotion. Some tend to be arrogant or braggadocio, which turns off almost everyone that might help a person who is trying to start, build or change her career. Others are so weak and timid in telling their own stories that others never even know that person is trying to advance her career.

In this book, Debby strikes the perfect balance, teaching the reader how he or she can deliver a confident, self-promoting story that engages the interest of others — and keeps the conversation going. Her advice is not only critically important but also practical and applicable.

Quite simply, I wish I'd known Debby's tried-and-true method decades ago.

It would've saved me years of wrong turns and dead ends as I developed my career as a university professor. And it would have given me a shortcut to success as I changed my career from teaching to professional speaking and writing.

Here's the good news: you don't have to go down the trial-and-error path to the career success you want. Simply read this invaluable book and apply its lessons. Get started now, and you'll be well on your way to telling your story *and* getting the career you want!

Dr. Alan Zimmerman

Author of *The Payoff Principle: Discover the 3 Secrets for Getting What You Want Out of Life and Work*

Introduction

What makes some people so much more successful in navigating their career paths than others? Why do some seem to constantly move forward while others stagnate? What makes the difference?

Think of the people you've met who are most successful in their chosen fields. When you first meet them, they capture your attention in a few short seconds, don't they? They are immediately credible. They quickly create curiosity so that you want to get to know them better and learn more about what they do. They have mastered the art of self-promotion.

I am an executive coach, keynote speaker and workshop leader. In these roles, I've had the opportunity to work with a wide variety of people over the last 13+ years.

My clients have ranged from C-level executives to people who have been laid off from their jobs, from lawyers to middle managers in large companies, from entrepreneurs to authors and from those nearing retirement age to students preparing to enter the workforce.

Over the years, I've realized that all of my clients, regardless of their title, status, age, gender or rank need to tell their stories in order to reach their career goals. In other words, each of them needs to be able to self-promote. I've also learned that nearly every one of them is less effective in promoting themselves and telling their stories than they could be and should be. In short, my work has shown me that few have mastered the critically important art of self-promotion. All of us have unique stories to tell, and it is those stories that set us apart.

Whenever I conduct workshops on The Art of Self-Promotion, the room fills to capacity. My individual coaching clients are also hungry for tools to help them tell their stories more effectively. People are eager to learn the art of self-promotion. They recognize the importance of telling their stories but are not sure how to do it. In addition, they bring baggage with them in the form of all of the experiences they have had with over-promoters — the people who promote themselves in an off-putting way.

When I ask clients and workshop participants to tell their stories, they often fall silent.

They're afraid and uncomfortable practicing the art of self-promotion. Often, they feel that self-promotion is somehow shameful and wrong.

My purpose in writing this book is three-fold. First, I want to shift the way you think about self-promotion. Simply by virtue of the fact that you are reading this book, I know you're interested in becoming a more effective self-promoter. I also know from my years coaching and training people in this arena that you likely have some deep-seated mindsets about self-promotion that are getting in the way of your effectiveness. I want to help you uncover those disempowering mindsets and begin to shift them toward beliefs that are more positive and empowering.

My second objective is to give you tools to help you craft your self-promotion story. While it's critically important to shift your mindset so that you feel empowered to self-promote, it is equally vital to know how to self-promote so that your efforts help you reach your career goals. It's one thing to think, "Yes, self-promotion is something I'd like to do," and another thing all together to know that you have the tools at your disposal to tell your story effectively. I want you to finish reading this book with those fundamental tools and skills.

Third and finally, I want you to walk away with a practical plan for promoting yourself in the most effective way to the people in the best positions to help you reach your individual career goals. Tools are great, but only if you implement them. I want to be sure you are armed with a self-promotion plan and the accountability you need to implement it.

Powerfully and comfortably telling your story will be the key to reaching your goals, regardless of whether you seek a new job in your current field, a promotion within your organization, a larger, more ideal client base or a new career path entirely. People who master the art of self-promotion are those who find themselves successful in every arena. They are at the top of their fields, have the most success in interviews, develop more clients, get the best assignments and are the most quickly promoted.

So, let's dive in, figure out what stops you from self-promoting and get those roadblocks out of the way so you can learn to tell your story and transform your career.

Chapter One

The What and Why of Self-Promotion

As I said, I am an executive coach, keynote speaker and workshop leader. I am also a former practicing lawyer. Often, when I meet new people, one of the first things I am asked is how I ended up doing what I do for a living.

Believe it or not, the journey began when I was in fourth grade. I was cast to play Annie in our school musical, *Annie Get Your Gun*. This was a really exciting opportunity for me. I was thrilled that I landed the lead role until I found out that the girl who played Annie had to sing a solo in front of the whole school. It was then I discovered that I am not a naturally gifted singer.

For those of you who are not familiar with *Annie Get Your Gun*, one of the most well-known songs from the musical includes a refrain of "Anything you can do, I can do better. I can do anything better than you."[1]

Annie Oakley

I took this line as my anthem and in spite of my lack of natural singing talent, I persevered and performed in the role of Annie in front of my schoolmates and family members. And, although my musical theatre career came to a screeching halt, I learned that I loved being on stage.

So, at age nine, I had to coach myself into a new career path. I detoured from the stage and after graduating from high school in a suburb of Atlanta, I went to Duke University where I majored in public policy. I then worked briefly as a management consultant with Bain & Company. Although I loved my clients and colleagues at Bain, I quickly figured out that heavy analytical work was not something I wanted to do for the long haul.

Having eliminated number crunching as well as musical theatre from my possible career list, I went back to Duke in the late 80's and got my law degree. This set me on a 16-year trajectory of practicing corporate, technology and trademark law. I began working with a large law firm back in my hometown of Atlanta and later started and ran my own practice. Over the years, I represented companies of all sizes and stages in a variety of industries. I met a tremendous number of really talented people and crafted legal strategies to help them grow their businesses.

While I enjoyed certain aspects of practicing law, I always felt that something was missing. I most enjoyed working with clients, meeting new people, learning about businesses and helping clients set goals. In fact, during the time I had my own law practice, I was often out networking and meeting new people in an effort to build my client base. This is when I began honing my own self-promotion skills, sharing the pieces of my story that made me unique in my chosen field. During this time I also found my true calling: coaching.

While networking, I began meeting coaches. I was intrigued by how they described their work and by the idea of partnering with people to help them reach their goals and become more successful. I realized that I could leverage everything I had learned about self-promotion, everything I had learned about working with people, and everything I had learned about running a business, but in a completely different way. So I changed careers again.

In 2002, I hired a coach for myself. I went through coach training and certification with the Coaches' Training Institute, and I founded my company, Novateur Partners. As of the writing of this book, I've been doing this work for almost 14 years. I coach and train people all over the United States and just this year, I led my first training abroad.

I work one-on-one with individuals, and I also speak and conduct workshops for groups, both small and large.

I love that I get to partner with people so that they reach their goals more quickly and easily than they would have without coaching. And, I love helping my clients tell their stories more effectively and seeing them transform their careers.

I also love that as a keynote speaker and workshop leader, I've found a way to get myself back "on stage" without ever having to sing another solo!

Tell Your Story to Transform Your Career

I tell a version of that story every time I begin a self-promotion workshop. When I finish, I always ask the workshop participants what they notice in hearing my monologue. They tell me that I made them laugh, that I shared my credentials without being boring, that I engaged them, and that I circled back so that I ended where I began.

All of those observations are accurate. In addition, and perhaps most importantly, I told a story — a self-promotion story. I comfortably, artfully and confidently told a self-promotion story that allowed me to weave in all my credentials and all of my relevant experience. I gave my audience the story version of my resume, and I did it with my own unique twist. I established credibility while creating curiosity so that my audience stayed engaged.

Self-promotion is about being authentic, confident and proud.

At the core, self-promotion is simply being able to tell your story in your own voice. It's using your passions, your interests, your personality, and your humor to communicate your value to those who need to know who you are, what you do, and how well you do it. Self-promotion is about being authentic, confident and proud. It's also about tempering your pride with humility so you don't find yourself going over the top.

Self-Promotion Fundamentals

✓ What it is	✗ What it is NOT
Telling Your Story	Selling Yourself
Being Authentic	Putting on a Persona
Positivity	Disparaging Others
Confidence	Arrogance
Showcasing Your Strengths	Bragging
Highlighting Your Accomplishments	Oversharing and Overpowering
Establishing Your Credibility	Regurgitating Your Resume
Creating Curiosity	Reciting a Boring, Canned Speech
Leveraging Your Experiences	Embellishing the Truth

That's what this book is all about. How can you learn to tell your story? How can you effectively, comfortably and confidently communicate your value? How can you master the art of self-promotion?

Before we delve into how you can become a more effective self-promoter, I'd like to help you hone in on how mastering the art of self-promotion could help you transform your career.

Ask yourself, "How could telling my story more effectively help *me* in my career? If I were better at self-promotion, what would the impact be?"

There are many possible answers — many ways that self-promotion could be a game-changer for your career. Maybe you need to develop more business for yourself or your company. If you want to develop business, people need to know who you are and what you do.

Perhaps you can identify with David. David is a CPA who works in a small accounting firm. When I began coaching David, I asked him how being a more effective self-promoter could help him. He told me that originating and maintaining a robust roster of clients is critical to success at his firm. In fact, developing more business was the final barrier that stood between David and partnership at his CPA firm.

Or, maybe you're an entrepreneur. Cultivating a flourishing network that generates business is critical to your company's success and your continued ability to put food on the table. Like my client, Josie, who owns an architectural design firm, client development is something you need to be doing all the time if you want to keep the doors open. Those who master the art of self-promotion create strong relationships that lead to increased business.

Perhaps you see that being a more effective self-promoter will ensure that your employer and your clients know they can trust you. You want them to have confidence in you and your work. You may identify with Mike. Mike worked tirelessly for his company but because of several reorganizations within his department, no one knew what he was doing or how he contributed. His newest boss had no idea that Mike was the superstar in the department, so Mike needed to learn to tell his story. As with Mike, effective self-promotion is your vehicle for telling your story so that your bosses and clients know they can rely on you and your skills. Self-promotion is a way you can increase your credibility.

Of course, if you're job hunting or contemplating a change in your career path, self-promotion is a necessity. How you tell your story is an important influence on your job hunting success. I worked with Abby, a seasoned staffing company executive, who wanted to change her career path at mid-life. By telling her story with more passion and authenticity, she opened the door to opportunities in her newly chosen field.

Maybe you want more acknowledgement or to be given more plumb assignments at work. Self-promotion is important in these situations, too. If you effectively promote yourself, you will be able to build your brand.

Those with a need to know will be familiar with you and what you bring to the table. Like my client, Ron, a manager in a payment processing company, you may see that effective self-promotion will move you from toiling in the background to playing on the front lines in your company.

These are just some of the ways that being an effective self-promoter can help you transform your career path and move forward toward your goals. Based on what I've seen and heard from my coaching clients and workshop audiences, I think we can agree that effective self-promotion is a necessary component of any good career development plan.

A Note to C-level Executives

If you are currently at the C-level within your organization and you have picked up this book, you may be thinking that it is not aimed at you. You may not believe that self-promotion applies to you given where you are in your career trajectory. While it's true that you probably don't have traditional performance reviews and you may not be looking to change jobs or career paths, you still need to be thinking about how you promote yourself and your organization.

Admittedly, when I began writing this book, I did so with the clear conviction that mastering the art of self-promotion is critical to anyone embarking on a career, changing careers, or pursuing the next rung on a career ladder (or jungle gym, as Sheryl Sandberg describes it)[2]. However, at that point, I hadn't explicitly considered the applicability of these concepts to those of you who are at the pinnacle of your careers. That is until my husband and colleague, Dan Sheedy, asked me whether I was writing a C-level self-promotion section for this book. Like me, Dan coaches a number of C-level executives, and he reminded me of the importance of self-promotion to those of you who are running organizations.

There are multiple ways in which the concepts in this book apply to you. First, we're all accountable to someone. Although you may not have a boss in the traditional sense, you likely report to a board of directors or have clients or shareholders to whom you are accountable. For you to continue to be successful in your role, they need to know what you are doing, how you are doing it and why you continue to be the right person for the job.

Second, you're a role model for everyone else in your organization. If you are adept at telling your story (and the company's story), then you are setting a great example for others who need and want to do the same.

When your company's employees consider whether self-promotion is appropriate, they will be looking to you for guidance. How you talk about your accomplishments, and those of the company, will influence how your company's employees tell their individual stories and the company's story when they are out marketing your organization's products or services.

Third, when you are adept at self-promotion, it benefits your company's brand and reputation. As a top executive in your company, you influence the brand more than anyone else. You are the face of the organization, so the way you tell your story and the company's story is critical to continued growth and success. What are your company's strengths? What has your organization accomplished? What is the company passionate about and committed to? What is the company's history and how is it different from other organizations? What is your brand and how can you reinforce that brand?

Finally, you should read this book because your employees should read this book. Self-promotion is an art that you and your leadership team should encourage your employees to master. When the people in your organization can tell their stories effectively, everyone benefits.

Armed with a clear, powerful story, your company's leadership team is better able to acquire the information it needs to hire and promote the best people.

As Jim Collins said in *Good to Great*, you have much higher odds of getting "the right people on your bus."[3] Your company's bottom line is enhanced because your team attracts more clients and develops more business. If your organization's story is being told effectively, good things will happen.

The benefits of mastering the art of self-promotion are many, not only for you, but also for the other individuals in your organization and your company as a whole.

To Know

- Self-promotion is all about telling your story in your own voice; leveraging your passion, your personality and your sense of humor to confidently communicate your value to others.
- Mastering the art of self-promotion can transform any career through (i) increased business/client development, (ii) enhanced credibility and brand recognition, and (iii) improved job interview performance.
- Whether you are seeking your first job or are at the pinnacle of your career, mastering the art of self-promotion pays dividends.

To Explore

- ❑ Consider the following questions: (i) How could telling my story more effectively help me in my career; and (ii) What would the impact be if I mastered the art of self-promotion?

- ❑ If you are a C-level executive, ask yourself: How could masterfully telling my story and my company's story affect our brand, our sales and the organization's bottom line?

Chapter Two

It's All in Your Mind

Given that self-promotion plays such a key part in career development, what stops you from doing it? What are the roadblocks that prevent you from self-promoting or from being as effective at it as you'd like to be?

When I ask audiences this question, I get a variety of answers. Invariably someone says that modesty keeps them from self-promoting. They want to appear modest, rather than boastful. People also point out that it's difficult to know when the time is right for self-promotion. They don't feel that they can gauge when self-promotion is appropriate.

Others point out that it is impossible to effectively self-promote if you don't know what to say. They can identify opportunities for telling their stories but can't find the right words in the moment. Still others point to a lack of confidence.

They don't feel comfortable telling their stories or feel unsure about how their stories will be received. And finally, many express a concern that they do not know how much and which information to share. How much is too much in self-promotion?

Do you notice a trend in these answers? Lack of knowledge is often the barrier to effective self-promotion. We don't do it because we do not have all the answers. In other words, the biggest single reason that we fail to self-promote or to self-promote as effectively as we could is because we are tied up in our own heads. We worry about what to include, how it will be received, what the other person is thinking and what the rules of the game might be.

The fundamental reason that we don't self-promote is that in the absence of knowledge, we make assumptions. Then, based on those assumptions, we adopt beliefs about self-promotion that stop us from telling our stories. The roadblocks are all in your mind. Mastering the art of self-promotion boils down to shifting your mindset.

Assumptions and Beliefs

Let's talk a little bit about mindsets generally before we move into looking at your specific mindsets about self-promotion. First, it's important to note that we all hold mindsets about lots and lots of different things.

We hold mindsets about what it's like to live in different places in the world — even if we've never visited those places. We hold mindsets about certain colleges and universities and the types of people who attend those schools. We hold mindsets about the people we work with. We see some as competent and others as less so.

A mindset is the assumptions and beliefs you hold that shape the actions you see as possible.

We form beliefs and make judgments about all kinds of things. And that's really all a mindset is. A mindset is the assumptions and beliefs you hold that shape the actions you see as possible. According to thefreedictionary.com, a mindset is "a fixed mental attitude or disposition that predetermines a person's responses and interpretations of situations."[4]

If you have an empowering mindset about something, you see a whole universe of actions as possible. If you have a disempowering mindset — or what I would call a negative mindset — about something, that mindset will narrow the set of actions you believe are possible. Your mindset determines your responses and interpretations.

Let's explore an example. Suppose Roxanne has worked with me as an administrative assistant for a number of years. She is smart, terrifically competent, always on time and very responsive. I know her well, and she is a pleasure to interact with every day. Given her track record, over the years I've grown to trust her implicitly. I hold a mindset of trust about working with her.

With this mindset, there is a whole universe of possible ways Roxanne can help me do my job better. She can make travel plans, handle paperwork, return calls on my behalf, interact with my clients and manage my calendar.

Now let's say that Roxanne moves to another state, and I am assigned to work with Jeannie, another administrative assistant at the company. We'll assume that I've never worked directly with Jeannie, but I have heard some negative feedback about her and her work. Because of what I have heard, I adopt a mindset of distrust about working with Jeannie.

As a result, I see a very limited set of options for how we can work together. With this negative mindset in place, I am not going to delegate as much or feel that I can hand over as much responsibility. There are a lot of tasks that I would like an assistant to help me do that I am going to end up doing myself because of this limiting mindset. Much less is possible, and I may not even give Jeannie a fair chance.

Through this example, you can see how powerful a given mindset can be. The mindsets we hold about any particular person or thing will shape the actions we see as possible in relation to that subject. If we hold a positive mindset, much is possible. If we hold a negative or limiting mindset, there are fewer options available to us.

I like to think of mindsets as being similar to the tabs of commands you find in Microsoft® products. For example, if I am using Microsoft Outlook® to compose an email, and I want to change the format of the text in my message, I can see those options on the "Message" tab (at least that's true in the version of Outlook I am currently using). If I try to format the text from another tab, those options are simply not available. If I select a different tab, I don't see those options as possible.

For example on the "Insert" tab, I will see other available options such as "Signature" and "Attach File" but not the option to format the text in my message. Each tab has a limited set of available options. Similarly, there are only certain options available when you hold a particular mindset.

It's important to note that every mindset has a price and a payoff. There will be things that we give up by holding a certain mindset, and there is something we get. Sometimes the thing that we get doesn't seem like something we would necessarily want, but it keeps us safe or comfortable.

Again, think back to the administrative assistant example. Holding a negative mindset about Jeannie, the new assistant, means I delegate less. More work stays on my plate which, for me, is an undesirable outcome. I work longer and harder than ever before. However, by keeping more of the work to myself, I also get a sense of safety.

If I don't delegate to Jeannie as a result of my mindset of distrust, then she cannot mess anything up. I'm busier than I'd like to be, but I'm also safe. That's the price and the pay-off.

Making the Unconscious Conscious

Let's turn back to self-promotion now. We all hold certain mindsets about self-promotion. The mindsets you currently hold about self-promotion affect how and whether you tell your story, just as the mindset I held about my new assistant, Jeannie, affected how I interacted with and delegated to her.

Holding onto your current, limiting mindsets about self-promotion may have a payoff of keeping you safe. You tell yourself that if you don't talk to your boss about your accomplishments and goals, then you haven't put yourself out there where you're vulnerable to judgment and feedback. You are safe. However, the price of that mindset is that you don't get the benefit of having your boss know what you are accomplishing and factoring that into his analysis for a promotion or raise.

Similarly, if you are job hunting and don't specifically speak about your vast experience, your considerable expertise and your high degree of passion for the work, no one can see you as arrogant or as an over-promoter. You get to play it safe. However, if you stay silent, your interviewers won't learn how you would bring value to their organization.

See how this works? For every mindset there is a price and a payoff.

Some of the mindsets we hold are conscious and some are unconscious. When we hold a conscious mindset, we're aware of what we believe about something. We know what we think about that subject. If we choose to believe something else, we have the ability to intentionally shift our thinking. A conscious mindset allows us to clearly see that there is a price and a payoff associated with it.

On the other hand, our unconscious mindsets are, by definition, not readily known to us. As a result, they pose a greater danger. They lurk in the dark corners of our minds and grow there, becoming bigger and more powerful with each passing day. We are unaware of the price we are paying for holding those mindsets. Without being conscious of the mindsets we hold, it is impossible to shift or disarm them.

Therefore, being conscious of our mindsets, positive or negative, is critical to making the shifts that transform careers. We have to acknowledge our conscious mindsets and work to bring our unconscious mindsets to the surface.

As you've been reading this section on mindsets, I bet you've been thinking about the mindset or mindsets you currently hold about self-promotion. While we're on the subject, what *are* the mindsets you currently hold about self-promotion? What mindsets do you have about people who are self-promoters? Dig deeply. If you can move beyond the surface, perhaps you will uncover a previously unconscious mindset that you've been holding.

I'd also like you to think about what the price of those mindsets may be. What limitations do you face because of your current mindsets? How do your mindsets limit your self-promotion activities? How have your mindsets kept you stuck in your career path?

Now, focus for a moment on the payoffs. What do you get from the mindsets you currently hold? What are the benefits? Remember that the benefits don't always feel like benefits at first. Peel the onion and go deep. What am I getting from the mindsets I hold about self-promotion? Is it something tangible? Or perhaps it's something intangible, like safety?

Given what you now know about mindsets, it should be clear to you that the assumptions and beliefs you hold about self-promotion will shape the actions you take or don't take in promoting yourself to those who can impact your career. Your mindsets will either empower you or limit you.

To Know

- Lack of knowledge often stops us from self-promoting. We don't know enough about how, when and to whom to tell our stories. In the absence of knowledge we form unfounded beliefs and those beliefs stop us in our tracks.
- A mindset is the assumptions and beliefs you hold that shape the actions you see as possible. We hold mindsets about all types of things including self-promotion.
- Every mindset has a price and a payoff.
- Your mindsets about self-promotion will either empower or limit your career success.

To Explore

- ❑ What are the mindsets I currently hold about self-promotion?
- ❑ What do I believe about people who are self-promoters?
- ❑ How do my mindsets about self-promotion affect my actions?
- ❑ What is the payoff I get from holding the mindsets I hold?

Chapter Three

Shift Your Thinking

If I could poll all of you who are reading this book, much as I poll my audiences when I am speaking on this subject, I would find a variety of mindsets about self-promotion, most of them negative. As I mentioned, I have three main objectives in this book. The first is to shift how you are currently thinking about self-promotion.

I want to help you get past those roadblocks and negative images that the term "self-promotion" conjures up for you. Because we have all had experience with an over-promoter, we tend to flinch at promoting ourselves.

In fact, when you read the word "over-promoter," I bet you immediately know the person I am talking about. I would venture a guess that the image of someone in particular is coming to mind right now as you read these words. Yep. That person was a self-promoter alright, a self-promoter of the worst kind.

And after experiencing his brand of self-promotion, you probably decided that it simply wasn't for you. Better to stay silent than to run the risk of becoming "that guy" or "that woman."

It's understandable that you don't want to become an over-promoter and let me assure you now that you are not in any danger. How do I know that? I know it because you are reading this book. In fact, if you were even close to going over the top, you would certainly not have picked up this book. If you were already "that guy" or "that woman" you would never be attracted to a book entitled *The Art of Self-Promotion*, would you? After all, if you were "that guy" or "that woman" you would be confident in your own knowledge about self-promotion. Therefore, since you are reading this book, you have no need to worry about becoming an over-promoter.

Although I want to help you get the image of the over-promoters you were picturing out of your head for good, for a moment, I'd like you to think about those people and the beliefs you've formed based on those interactions. What other mindsets do you hold about self-promotion and people who are self-promoters?

Over the years, I have heard them all. Do any of these mindsets resonate with you?

- "Self-promoters are arrogant—you're full of yourself or conceited if you self-promote."
- "Self-promotion shouldn't be necessary because I should be rewarded for the work I do without having to tell people about it. That's fair, right?"
- "I think self-promotion is less effective than if other people tell my story."
- "Actions speak louder than words."
- "There's a thin line between promoting and bragging, so at some point you cross the line."
- "Self-promotion is uncomfortable. It's outside my comfort zone."

Those are just a few examples of the many negative mindsets I have heard about self-promotion.

Based on the negative mindsets people hold about self-promotion, there are two overarching themes. The first is that everything will work out fairly. If we do good work, we should not have to self-promote. We should be justly rewarded for a job well done. The second theme is that we believe self-promotion is not socially acceptable. In other words, society, culture, our families and our upbringing have all conditioned us to believe that it's not okay for us to promote ourselves, and as a result, we're not comfortable doing so. Let's delve into both of those themes.

Fundamental Fairness

First, how about this idea that the workplace operates fairly, and we will be justly rewarded for good work? This concept resonates with many of us because we have a fundamental belief in fairness. If we do a good job, we should be recognized. Our good work should be noticed and appropriately rewarded.

This concept rests on the theory that life is fair, and that the work world operates in a fair and equitable manner. It relies on the idea that other people — our bosses, prospective clients, future employers and other influential people — will become aware of our accomplishments and then fairly and justly make decisions about our employability, our merit, our trustworthiness and our potential based on this information.

I wish that I could tell you that things would always work out fairly and that if you do a good job, you will be recognized and properly rewarded. Class dismissed.

That would be great, but unfortunately, it's not that simple. In today's world, for a number of reasons, this theory doesn't hold up.

First of all, the world is simply not fair all the time. People don't always reward us in direct proportion to our actual performance and contribution. We all know someone who has been passed over for a promotion and later learns that the promotion went to someone whose performance was not as good.

I recently heard a story that illustrates this point. Harris consistently did terrific work in his role as a manager in the training department at a large telecommunications company. He put in long hours, was responsive to client requests and managed his team effectively so that they produced high quality results. His colleague and fellow manager, Andy, was relatively well-regarded in his role too, although most people at the company agreed that Harris was the stronger overall performer.

You can imagine Harris' surprise when Andy was promoted to senior manager before he was. As it turns out, Harris was working under the assumption that things would be fair and that his reward would be in direct proportion to his performance. Andy, on the other hand, had been vocal about his accomplishments and his desire to move up to senior manager. Although Andy's work wasn't quite as good, he was promoted because he spoke up for himself and created buzz, while Harris did not.

Second, the people we work with are exceedingly busy and are inundated with information. It's very difficult for your boss, your boss' boss or your prospects to keep track of what you do and whether what you do is worthy of reward. What you're doing and how well you're doing it is a top priority for you, but it's typically not the most important thing to anyone else.

Corporate leaders, and all of us in business, have other things to think about, other things to deal with. Your boss may be too busy considering whether to let someone go due to underperformance to notice your incredible work on your latest project. A prospective client may not make time to do the research required to learn more about your company's track record of success and may instead rely upon the testimonials handed to him by another company vying for his business.

One of my clients, Paige, had to meet this truth head on in her job. Paige worked for a small insurance brokerage firm for many years as an administrative assistant. In that role, she reported directly to the firm's founder, Derek, and had a solid relationship with him. As time passed, she yearned to grow professionally and spoke to Derek about this desire. When Derek decided that the company was ready to have a full-time office manager, he offered the opportunity to Paige.

Paige was thrilled and embraced her new role fully and passionately. She spent long days working out issues between staff members, ordering supplies, overseeing the construction of the office expansion, ensuring that invoices were paid, getting client bills sent out on time, and in short, keeping the entire office running smoothly. Paige was solving the company's myriad problems before they ever reached Derek's radar. She felt that she was really excelling in her new role.

When it came time for her first performance review in her new role, Paige was excited. She "knew" she would receive kudos for a job well-done and hoped to get a raise. She looked forward to hearing praise for her hard work and confidently stepped into Derek's office on the appointed day and time.

Derek began their conversation by saying that he'd really like to give Paige her performance review but that unfortunately he could not. Crestfallen, Paige looked at him with confusion. He continued, saying that he could not review her because he had no idea what she had been doing all those months!

His words could certainly launch me into a diatribe about his managerial skills (any decent manager should have more than a mere idea of what his/her employees are doing). However, his inactions did not change the fact that Paige had done such a poor job (no job really) of promoting herself to Derek and letting him know what she had been doing. Derek had no idea about the problems she was solving and the pro-active steps she was taking to ensure that the company operated smoothly. He did not have the information he needed to review her.

You can imagine her disappointment. You can also imagine that a large portion of our coaching focused on how she could promote herself to Derek and other company leaders in the future so that this scenario never, ever repeated itself. Paige had assumed that because she had worked so hard, she would be fairly evaluated and compensated. Because of this belief, she had overlooked the need to self-promote or tell Derek her story.

The third reason the fairness theory does not hold up is that we live in a time of mobility in the workforce. The person that you report to today may not be the person you report to next week, next month or next year. As a result of internal corporate changes and reorganizations, you may find yourself with a blank slate — somebody who doesn't know who you are, how you do what you do or how you contribute to the organization.

Many of my coaching clients have told me about changes in their leadership. They say, "I got a new boss last week, what should I tell her?" Your new boss or your division's new leader comes in without any history. She doesn't know your track record of success and likely has no idea where your strengths lie. The blank slate is both a challenge and an opportunity.

Rob is a great example of the importance of taking pro-active steps to tell your story when your leadership changes. Rob recently told me that he wanted to renegotiate his arrangement with the human resources consulting company he had been working for over the last 10 years. He wanted more flexibility, more freedom to explore some of his other interests and a slightly different set of responsibilities. The CEO of Rob's company was relatively new to the role, and as a result, he had only known Rob for the few months of his tenure. The CEO did not know Rob's rich history with the company, nor was he aware of all of the many contributions Rob had made over the years.

Rob is savvy. Rob knew that for the CEO to approve his proposed new working arrangement, he would need to fully understand Rob's role and contributions over time. Without that context, it would be impossible for the CEO to adequately value Rob and to make a reasoned decision about how the company should treat him.

Rob did what any smart self-promoter would do. He made a list of all of his accomplishments over the years. He focused special attention on the specific actions he took and the results he achieved that did not get directly reflected in the company's bottom line. He made sure that the CEO knew all about the initiatives he started, the ideas he piloted and the teams he built.

Once Rob had that list compiled, he was ready to present his proposal to the CEO. Then, and only then, was Rob prepared to give the CEO the information and context he needed to evaluate his proposed new role. Rob told his story so that the CEO would have all the facts and background he needed. And, guess what? With little negotiation, the CEO approved Rob's plan. By effectively promoting himself, Rob was able to achieve the result he sought. Rather than assuming he would be rewarded for all his hard work over the years, Rob told his story and ensured his own success.

The moral of the stories in this section should be clear — it is NOT safe to assume that the world is fair or that if you keep your head down and do a good job you will be justly rewarded. You must self-promote; you must tell your story.

The Discomfort Zone

The second theme of the negative mindsets that many people hold about self-promotion is that it's uncomfortable. We simply do not feel good about telling our own stories and talking about our accomplishments. This is a deeply, and nearly universally, held mindset. The vast majority of us feel that self-promotion is uncomfortable and that there is something socially unacceptable about it. As a result, we don't do it. We stay within our comfort zones. We buy into the mindsets that society, our culture, our schools, our parents and our contemporaries have sold us, and we hold back.

Lindsay, now a successful executive in the pharmaceutical industry, shared with me that she remembered a scene from elementary school that shaped her views on self-promotion. She came home from school with the results of an important spelling test. She had gotten 100% on the test and was really excited to tell her Mom. She remembers running into the house and shouting, "Mommy, Mommy, look I got a 100 on my test!" She then remembers her Mom saying, "Oh honey, that's wonderful. I'm glad you're excited, and I'm excited too. But remember, don't tell everybody at school because it will make them feel badly if they didn't get 100 too."

Like Lindsay, we have all received those kinds of messages at some point in our lives and likely we've internalized them. Those internalized messages have, in turn, shaped our mindsets about self-promotion and caused us to feel uncomfortable telling our stories. We don't want to do it because we don't think it's socially acceptable.

Although I used to hold back on my own self-promotion for similar reasons, I have worked hard to push past those internal limitations. While it is never my aim to make others feel bad, I am not embarrassed or ashamed to promote myself. Over the years, I've learned that I can strike a balance between telling my story and going over the top. That balance allows me to effectively self-promote without making others feel bad at all.

In fact, others are often inspired by someone who has mastered the art of self-promotion.

This is where humility comes into play. Often we tell ourselves that it's better to be quiet and to be viewed as humble, than to raise our voices and self-promote. No doubt humility is important. It's a wonderful characteristic that many of us strive to cultivate and maintain. It is not, however, the criteria on which we are typically judged for employment, client engagements, promotions or other career moves.

In fact, others are often inspired by someone who has mastered the art of self-promotion.

Take a moment and list the top five personal characteristics of the person who will be hired for the job you want, who will receive the promotion you seek, or who will enroll the client you are courting. Is humility on that list? I bet it's not. No doubt you listed things like responsive, detail-oriented, strategic, personable or loyal.

While it is almost certainly not on the list of qualities needed for your next career move, humility is the balance. Humility will keep you from becoming an over-promoter. If you have the right amount of humility, you can promote yourself and not cross that line. You can tell your story and transform your career comfortably and confidently. Note I said "confidently" and not "arrogantly." That is because we can use our humility to balance out our self-promotion.

The end product is a self-promotion story that is both compelling and powerful — a story that helps us move forward and achieve our career goals.

Not Me; I'm Different

You may be thinking that this is all well and good for the majority of people but not for you. Perhaps you are thinking that the analysis is different for you because of your gender, because you come from a particular area of the country or because of your cultural background. Let me address those concerns right here, right now.

First, let's talk about self-promotion for women versus self-promotion for men. It is true that society and upbringing often condition women to be even more reluctant to self-promote than men. However, in my work, I have found that most men also struggle with the feeling that self-promotion is uncomfortable or unacceptable. I can also think of as many women as men that I've personally encountered who are effective self-promoters and who are completely comfortable singing their own praises. While it is certainly difficult for women to overcome these negative mindsets, it is often equally difficult for men.

Second, let's address regional differences. I live in the South, and it's true that there is probably more self-promotion going on in a Wall Street firm than in a small southern company. From a historical perspective, the South certainly has a more ingrained philosophy of traditional gentility. However, even with that historical perspective as a backdrop, business is business, and to be successful in your career, you must tell your story. Where, when and how you tell it may be different in Charlotte than it is in Chicago, but tell it you must.

Finally, let's tackle cultural norms. I have presented my self-promotion workshop to a number of cohorts of engineering master's students at Duke University.[5] Many of the students are international and often will approach me after the program to share their stories. The students tell me that Asian cultures in particular frown on self-promotion and that their reluctance to self-promote runs deep as a result.

Li approached me after one of these programs and expressed her concerns about promoting herself. I asked Li whether she planned to return to her home country of China to work after receiving her master's degree or whether she was planning to work in the U.S. Like most of the students I have spoken with, Li wanted to work in the United States or take a job in her home country with a U.S.-based company upon graduation. As a result, self-promotion is a critical success factor for Li and her fellow students during the interview process and remains critical as they move forward in their careers.

Regardless of your cultural background, being able to effectively tell your story is imperative if you want to be successful in a U.S. company.

Mindsets originate from many different sources – culture, gender, family of origin, geographic region, educational background. It is important for you to uncover, confront and overcome your own personal limiting mindsets so that you can tell your story. Doing so does not mean abandoning your cultural, regional or gender identity. Rather it means finding a way to honor who you are while also expanding your individual comfort zone.

To Know

- ❑ Good work doesn't always lead to just rewards. The workplace is not always fair.
- ❑ Your bosses, clients and prospects are often too busy to keep track of your accomplishments so you must tell them.
- ❑ You may find yourself with a new boss or leader. That clean slate can seem like a challenge but is also an opportunity. By telling your story you maximize the opportunity.
- ❑ Others are inspired by someone who has mastered the art of self-promotion.
- ❑ You must unearth, confront and overcome your self-limiting mindsets in order to master self-promotion.

To Explore

- ❑ What beliefs underlie my current mindsets about self-promotion?
- ❑ Where does my negative mindset come from? Is there a story in my past from which it originates?
- ❑ How does my gender, geography or culture affect my beliefs about self-promotion?

Chapter Four

You've Got the Power

Remember back in Chapter One when I asked you how self-promotion could transform your career? Remind yourself of your answer. Whether you're looking for your first job, transitioning your career path, hunting for new clients or building your brand within your current organization, self-promotion is critical to getting you where you want to go. You must tell your story effectively to achieve the success you desire, and chances are, you are not as effective as you could be.

You must tell your story effectively to achieve the success you desire, and chances are, you are not as effective as you could be.

In fact, it's safe to say that if you are reading this book, you can increase the effectiveness of your self-promotion. You can amp up the power of your self-promotion efforts. In other words, you can tell your story more effectively and with more confidence than you currently do.

The Self-Promotion Scale

Let's think about self-promotion on a scale of 0-10. On one end of the spectrum at zero, you are not promoting yourself or telling your story at all. At the other end of the spectrum at ten, you are a fabulous self-promoter. Your stories are on point, on target. You balance your story with just the right amount of humility so that you don't tip the scales over the edge. There is no danger of being perceived as an over-promoter. You are simply doing a wonderful job of effectively promoting yourself. You have mastered the art of self-promotion.

Now think about your own self-promotion. If you are like most people, your self-promotion efforts are probably hovering at around a 2-3 on that ten point scale. Interestingly though, we all tend to have an inflated sense of how well we are self-promoting. You would likely rate your self-promotion higher on the 0-10 scale than others would. It is very difficult for most of us to accurately gauge our own self-promotion efforts. Although we occasionally amp things up to a 4 or a 5, we typically hang out well below that point because we are so terrified of becoming an over-the-top, obnoxious over-promoter. We keep our self-promotion efforts in the safe zone so we can be assured that no one could possibly be offended.

In all likelihood, this is not even a conscious decision you are making. Typically, we keep our self-promotion efforts to a minimum because of those darn unconscious mindsets and in response to our own inner critical voice. As a result though, we are not nearly as effective as we could be in telling our own stories. In short, we have a lot of room to turn up the power of our self-promotion efforts before they cross the line. We can be far more effective in telling our stories without any risk of becoming over-promoters.

I remember checking out my own self-promotion efforts with a trusted colleague years ago. I feared that I was getting painfully close to the line and did not want to become an over-promoter, so I asked for his opinion. I was amazed to learn that I was hovering around a 5 on the 0-10 scale and that I still had lots of room to increase the power of my own self-promotion efforts. The feedback helped me realize that I could tell my story far more powerfully if only I could get out of my own way.

I want to encourage you to check this out by testing your self-promotion with someone in your life. This simple exercise will help you begin to gauge your current self-promotion story and give you a context for the remainder of what you will learn in this book. Here is what I suggest: Find a friend, colleague, coach or some other "willing victim." In other words, find someone who is willing to listen to your self-promotion story. Explain the self-promotion scale of 0-10 by reading your partner the short passage above.

Then ask your partner to time you. Give yourself 20 seconds to self-promote. Introduce yourself to your partner in this exercise the same way you would introduce yourself to someone you were meeting for the first time at a networking event. Tell them who you are and what you do in less than 20 seconds. Then, when you complete your 20-second self-promotion, ask your partner to give you a score on that 0-10 scale. You can ask your partner for additional feedback, but the main purpose is for you to get that number. Where does your self-promotion rank on that 0-10 scale?

When I speak on self-promotion, I ask audience members to pair up and engage in this exercise. How often do you think someone gets a 10 for their self-promotion efforts? Very, very rarely! In fact, I've been speaking on this subject for more than five years at the time of this writing, and so far only two people have ever scored a 10. Of course, I jokingly told each perfect 10 self-promoter that he could teach the rest of the workshop since he had apparently cracked the self-promotion code, but neither of the two took me up on that offer!

Typically, the vast majority of those in the room score a 5 or lower. A few people get scores between 6-8, but for everyone except the two perfect 10's, there is room to increase the power and effectiveness of everyone's self-promotion efforts.

All of us can more skillfully tell our stories. We all have one or more self-limiting mindsets that keep our self-promotion efforts from being as masterful as they could be.

Now that you have a better idea of how to gauge where your current self-promotion efforts score on the 1-10 scale, are you ready to increase the power and effectiveness of your self-promotion? Let's get started!

Building Blocks

I want to begin with the notion that you have the building blocks you need to master this art. We all know how to tell a story. In fact, we do it all the time for other people. We simply don't use those skills as effectively as we might in telling our own stories.

Several years ago, I was preparing to deliver a webinar for the Duke University Career Center, and I had a conversation about self-promotion with Bill Wright-Swadel, the Center's Executive Director. As we discussed self-promotion, Bill noted that typically the students who come into the Career Center have not learned the art of self-promotion. Although some do a better job than others, most need to tell their own stories more powerfully, and the Career Center staff teaches them how to do that.

Bill often converses with students about their job prospects, their interests and the status of their career searches. During those conversations, he may also ask a student about their friends' job searches. Bill said that in the course of those conversations, he's noticed the dichotomy between how a student naturally tells someone else's story and how that same student (before self-promotion training) tells her own story.

Karen is a great example of a student who began her career search as a less than masterful self-promoter. When Karen first came into the Career Center, Bill asked Karen about her friend, Connor. Based on what Bill told me about his interactions with his students, I imagine that Bill's conversation with Karen may have gone something like this: "Karen, I noticed that your friend, Connor, has applied to work as a consultant with X Co. From your perspective, what makes Connor a fit for that role?" Bill says that when he asks a student like Karen to talk about a friend, the student becomes very animated.

Karen may have said something like, "I'd love to tell you about Connor. Connor has a great analytical mind. Connor's a natural leader. He has a wonderful sense of humor. He is a computer science major, and this job calls for a lot of work with software and technology companies. He would be an ideal fit for this job." As Karen described Connor, she showed passion and enthusiasm. She gave examples, and she had terrific stories to tell that illustrate why Connor would be an ideal fit for the job.

Bill said that he then asked Karen about a job she had applied for. Again, I imagine Bill said something like, "So Karen, I see that you have applied for a job with Big Co. Tell me about you, what would make you a good fit for this job with Big Co.?" Bill said that when asked about herself, Karen, like many students, responded in a much less powerful, confident and passionate way. I imagine that Karen may have looked down at her shoes or up at the ceiling or someplace else in the room — anyplace but looking him in the eye. She likely looked back up uncomfortably and said something very non-descript, without a lot of enthusiasm, such as: "Well, you know I have done pretty well in school, and uh…I'm from the Midwest and the job is in the Midwest and uh..."

Bill said that often the students, like most of us, will stammer and stutter their way through their own stories, not saying much at all. When addressing the question about herself, Karen did not show the passion or enthusiasm she showed when talking about her friend Connor. Her tone was completely different. She didn't tell stories or give examples. She failed to self-promote. (That is, until the Career Center taught her how!)

The point is that we all know how to tell a story, and we do it naturally and beautifully when it's a story about someone else. We have all of the fundamental skills. But, when it's about ourselves, we get uncomfortable. We lose our footing. We become much less passionate, articulate, and clear.

If I asked you to tell me the story of your best friend and why she should get the job she has applied for or the promotion she seeks, you could easily tell me. You would tell me her story with enthusiasm, passion and excitement. You have the skillset. You know how to tell a story well. You simply need to become as effective at telling your own story as you are at telling someone else's story. You need to increase the power and effectiveness of your self-promotion.

Self-Promotion Super Hero

How do you go about increasing your storytelling power and reaching that perfect 10 on the self-promotion scale? Let's start by thinking about the self-promoter you know who would score a 10 on that scale — the person who has mastered the art of self-promotion. We've all encountered someone like that in our careers. This self-promotion super hero has found the ideal balance between effectively telling his story and going over the top. This person is not at all arrogant.

This person is so good at self-promotion that when he tells his story, it attracts you. You hear his story and you want to be friends with him. He is someone you want to work with, refer business to and get to know better. He is, for that moment, the most interesting man in the world. He is the Self-Promotion Super Hero.

To Know

- We all tend to have an inflated sense of how effectively we self-promote.
- In fact, most self-promotion efforts fall significantly lower on the effectiveness scale than they could and should.
- We need to check our efforts with others to validate the effectiveness of our self-promotion stories.
- You have the building blocks to master the art of self-promotion. You must simply learn to use your skills to tell your own stories.

To Explore

- ▢ Find a partner, and following the outline on page 46, check out your self-promotion efforts on the 0-10 scale.

- ▢ Think of someone you know who has mastered the art of self-promotion (your Self-Promotion Super Hero). What makes him or her masterful?

Chapter Five

Mindsets of the Masters

Think about your Self-Promotion Super Hero from the last chapter. What is it about that person and the way she promotes herself that works? How did she master the art of self-promotion?

Those questions lead us back to mindsets. Remember that mindsets are the assumptions and beliefs we hold that shape the actions we see as possible. To master the art of self-promotion, we must adopt the most empowering mindsets. Let's examine the mindsets of the masters. What do effective self-promoters assume and believe about themselves and about telling their stories?

The Seven Core Beliefs

1. **Effective self-promoters believe that telling their stories will transform their careers.**

Every effective self-promoter knows that she holds the key to her success. She is clear about the purpose of telling her story, and she knows that she is the best person to do it. She knows what her message is and to whom it must be delivered. She believes that self-promotion is a tool she can use to ensure that she stays in the driver's seat of her career in order to reach her career goals.

> Establish credibility and create curiosity – the two goals of every effective self-promotion effort.

Do you believe that telling your story is critical to your own success? If so, when you are telling your story, what are you trying to accomplish? What is your purpose or goal? Overall, the purpose or goal of any self-promotion is two-fold — first, to establish or further credibility, and second, to create curiosity. Establish credibility and create curiosity — the two goals of every effective self-promotion effort.

Initially, your goal is to give your conversation partner enough information so that he sees you as credible and wants to continue the conversation. If someone finds you credible, he is more likely to want to send business your way, hire you or promote you. If you aren't seen as credible, none of those outcomes is likely. Trust is a key factor in career success and credibility helps build that sense of trust.

Second, if what you say creates curiosity in your listener, that person is more likely to continue the conversation. He will ask you questions so that you can share more about yourself, your accomplishments and how you contribute. In short, the more curiosity you create, the longer the conversation will continue. The by-product of a longer conversation is a stronger connection. Longer conversations and stronger connections lead to an increased likelihood of creating or furthering the relationship between the people engaged in the conversation. And, as Susan Scott says in her book, *Fierce Conversations*, "The conversation is the relationship."[6]

Relationships are the foundation of your career path and the difference maker in job-hunting, business development and brand-building. When you tell your story effectively, you create and further your relationships, and you drive the transformation of your career.

2. **Effective self-promoters believe in the importance of being sincere and authentic in their storytelling.**

When you are considering your story, ask yourself "Am I really connected to what I am saying? Is it real? Am I speaking from my heart?" Authenticity is a key component of effective self-promotion.

When we're authentic and sincere, we come across as more confident and comfortable (more on that in a moment). Authenticity and sincerity are also critical for creating that connection I mentioned earlier.

Have you ever tried to connect with someone who was not being authentic? Maybe you can relate to an experience I have had many times at networking events. Often, I meet someone new at one of these events, and in the first few seconds it is apparent to me that they have adopted a "networking persona" for purposes of the event. They say the "right" things, but I walk away from the interaction with nothing more than some empty words and a business card. It feels as if I've just met the cardboard cutout version of this person. The real person isn't there and as a result no real connection can be made.

Without authenticity and sincerity, our self-promotion efforts are as two-dimensional as a cardboard cutout. Our words ring hollow and the people we meet feel that they have no connection with us. It's impossible to connect with someone unless they are being authentic.

This is critically important as we consider self-promotion, because we cannot forget that careers are made or broken by relationships or lack thereof. Careers are about relationships with people, and to build a successful career, you have to successfully connect with people.

The only way to successfully connect with people is by being authentic and sincere.

Therefore, the most effective self-promotion stories are authentic and the most effective self-promoters are sincere, real, down-to-earth storytellers. When you tell your story, be yourself. Bring your sense of humor, your personality, your unique way of being, and use these components as your guide. You don't have to try to be somebody else.

I've spoken with many seasoned professionals who admit to having tried to model themselves on someone else when they first began working. Take John, for example. When John first began practicing law, he accompanied Stephanie, a more senior lawyer from his firm, to court for a trial. He was dazzled by Stephanie's courtroom skills and the way she came across to the judge and jury. She really connected with them and was extremely effective as a result.

John decided then and there that to be successful in his litigation practice, he should adopt Stephanie's courtroom style. He would promote himself and his client's claims the way Stephanie promoted herself and her client's claims. John mistakenly assumed that because Stephanie's style was effective for her it would be equally effective for him. What he failed to realize is that Stephanie's courtroom style was effective for her because it was authentic. It was Stephanie's real self, whereas for John it was a persona.

John learned this quickly when he had his first trial. He strode into court armed with his version of Stephanie's courtroom style, expecting to have tremendous success. Instead, he failed miserably. He did not connect well with the judge or the jury. He felt like an imposter, and everyone in the courtroom immediately felt that he had adopted a persona and was inauthentic. He lost the case and learned an important lesson — being authentic is absolutely critical to creating connection. John quickly shed the Stephanie style and resumed being himself. The next time he went to court, he was more comfortable, more confident and more effective as a result.

When you're authentic, you are able to connect so that people get to know you and what you offer.

3. Effective self-promoters believe in telling their stories, not selling themselves.

Many people equate self-promotion with sales. Unfortunately, this mistaken association often leads to a huge roadblock to self-promotion success because most people do not want to be in "sales." In fact, many of us have strongly ingrained, negative mindsets around the concept of sales or selling.

We've all seen aggressive sales people on TV or in retail stores, and most professionals shy away from that image. If that is what sales is all about, then we certainly do not want to sell ourselves in that way. As a result, we shy away from telling our stories at all.

Effective self-promoters know that storytelling is not about selling at all. Note that the word is "storytelling" and not "storyselling." You do not have to sell yourself to be an effective self-promoter. There is a difference between telling and selling. In order to effectively promote yourself, you need to *tell* your story. You need to tell people about yourself, your experience and what you offer.

When we think of selling, we frequently think about trying to make something happen: "I will make them want to hire me." "If I sell myself well, they will have no choice but to promote me." In our minds, selling typically implies that the buyer may not think she needs or wants what the seller is selling, but the seller will make her buy it anyway.

On the other hand, *telling* is about sharing information. It's about sharing a story. It is about gifting your target audience with the best possible information, artifacts and evidence about you. The right people need to know what you do and how capably you do it so they can make an informed decision about what you offer.

For example, if your interviewer does not know about your unique set of experiences, skills and strengths, she is not likely to recommend that the company hire you. If your boss does not know of your accomplishments, he is not likely to promote you. If a prospective client has never heard of you, that company is not likely to bring their business to you. Similarly, if that company, your boss or a prospective client has heard of you but does not know what you do or how well you do it, it's equally unlikely that you will be hired, promoted or awarded the business.

Best-selling business author, Daniel H. Pink says, "The purpose is to offer something so compelling that it begins a conversation, brings the other person in as a participant, and eventually arrives at an outcome that appeals to both of you."[7] Self-promotion is not about selling anything. It is all about telling your story and starting a conversation.

4. **Effective self-promoters believe that preparation is critical.**

I cannot overstate the importance of this principle — preparation, preparation, preparation. If you are not prepared to talk about yourself or if you are not prepared to tell your story, you will be caught off guard and you will not be effective at promoting yourself.

Several years ago I began coaching Chris. At the time, Chris was a senior director in a global manufacturing company and had risen quickly in the organization.

He told me that for the past year, he had been leading a team that was working on a critically important, high-stakes project. The project had the ability to make a real impact on the company as a whole. About nine months into his work on this project, he attended a two-day meeting that pulled together company executives from across the organization.

His team had already produced some initial success on their initiative, and he was proud of the work they were doing. Chris said that about halfway through the first day of the two-day meeting, he found himself alone in an elevator with the company's CEO. Hopefully when you read this set-up you are thinking to yourself, "Wow…this is a career-changing opportunity!" Chris said he was thinking the same thing.

Unfortunately though, he found himself tongue tied and couldn't think of a single thing to say to the CEO in that moment. He drew a complete blank because he was unprepared. So, what did Chris do? He did what we would all do in that situation; he talked to the CEO about the weather! Now, talking about the weather isn't all bad. It doesn't leave a negative impression, but that's only because it does not really leave any impression at all. Once the CEO got out of the elevator at his floor, Chris said he wanted to bang himself on the head.

He knew, in that moment, that he had been given the opportunity to make a positive impression on the CEO, to tout the accomplishments of his team and to self-promote, and he blew it.

As our coaching engagement progressed, we spent some time talking about what had happened in the elevator with the CEO and the importance of being prepared to tell your story at any time. Chris recognized the import of preparation and began to consider what he would say if he ever had another opportunity like the one he'd missed out on previously. What would he say if he found himself alone with the CEO again? Although he thought that the odds were slim to none that he would ever get that chance again, he figured he should be prepared, just in case. Regardless of whether he had another opportunity to share it, Chris believed that preparing his self-promotion story for the CEO would be a valuable exercise.

Amazingly, and I promise that I am not making this up, he did have the opportunity to speak with the CEO one-on-one again later that year. The company held another cross-functional meeting, and Chris stepped out of the meeting room to return a call. When he did, he found himself standing face-to-face with the CEO who had also stepped out for a moment. This time instead of saying "How about this warm weather?" Chris was prepared.

He knew what to say and how he wanted to say it, so it was easy for him to speak to the CEO about the team he was leading, the initiative they were working on and the successes they had experienced to date. He was prepared and able to powerfully tell his story.

I asked him afterwards what the experience was like this time around. He told me that the preparation had made promoting himself easy and natural. He felt really good about the interaction and clear that he had said what he intended to say. He was able to have a positive impact on the CEO with his story as a result of his preparation. In fact, Chris' boss told him that the CEO praised Chris and his project team at a subsequent meeting of the company's senior leadership.

In the course of our coaching engagement, Chris prepared to speak with his company's CEO, and he also prepared for a number of different audiences and scenarios.

When preparing for self-promotion, it's important to consider your audience and context. We all have lots of different opportunities to promote ourselves. The story we tell in a formal networking setting or in a meeting with a prospective client is not necessarily the same story we would share at a neighborhood barbeque or when we meet someone on an airplane.

> When preparing for self-promotion, it's important to consider your audience and context.

Speaking of airplanes, I can't help but think about an experience I had several years ago.

That January, I took a day trip to New Orleans from Atlanta to speak at a conference. I took a very early flight out in the morning, spoke to the group at lunchtime and then immediately took a cab to the airport to head back home.

At about 3:30, when I got to the New Orleans airport, the Delta representative informed me that all flights into Atlanta had been cancelled for the remainder of the day in light of an incoming ice storm. I was very surprised and not at all pleased. Granted I'd heard about the impending weather (and if you know anything about the South, you know that when an ice storm is expected, everything shuts down immediately), but during my cab ride to the airport, I had spoken to my office manager back in Atlanta, and she said that the sun was still shining.

I asked the Delta agent what my options were (keep in mind that I didn't have so much as a toothbrush with me since I left in the morning thinking I was on a day trip). She told me that I could wait and Delta would fly me back to Atlanta in the morning, or I could take a Continental flight to Houston and then connect to a flight from Houston to Atlanta later that evening.

Well, I am no geography whiz but I do know that Houston is in the opposite direction when traveling from New Orleans to Atlanta, and while I was stumped as to why Continental was still flying when Delta was not, I figured what the heck? If I didn't take the flight to Houston, then I knew I was definitely spending the night in the New Orleans airport, and if I flew to Houston, then maybe, just maybe, I could get back to Atlanta that same evening.

So I flew to Houston. When I arrived, I had a long layover, so when I finally boarded the plane to Atlanta it was after 9:00 pm CT. I had been up since around 4:30 ET that morning to catch my early flight to New Orleans, so by that time, I was quite tired. I hunkered down and spent the first half of the flight to Atlanta sitting quietly, thinking and reading.

At about the halfway point between Houston and Atlanta, the gentleman sitting next to me said, "Are you always this quiet?" I laughed, and you would too if you knew me, because quiet is not how I am typically described. I said no and told him the short version of the story of my day. He chuckled at my saga and then asked me what I did for a living. I told him about my work, and we ended up in a spirited conversation about leadership, coaching and professional development that lasted until we landed back in Atlanta.

As it turned out, he worked in Houston and was traveling to Atlanta on business. He was keenly interested in coaching and leadership development and could not wait to get back to Houston to introduce me to the people in his company in charge of their coaching and leadership development initiatives. He was a great connection for me and my business. I have coached some of his company's top level executives, and he has introduced me to several other opportunities over the years.

Even though I was exhausted, I was able to effectively tell him my story because I was prepared. Had I not prepared in advance for just such a moment, an opportunity would have been lost. The moral of the story is that all of us need to be ready any time and all the time to promote ourselves.

Preparation includes thinking ahead about when an opportunity might arise to tell your story, and it also includes doing research when you know an opportunity is coming up. If you know you have a chance to interview for a particular job or project, pitch a prospective client or attend a networking event, do your homework beforehand. Learn as much as possible about your audience in advance so that you can tailor your self-promotion story to the group, to an individual's personal style and to the context of your interaction.

As you prepare your self-promotion, you must also be wary of the jargon trap. We often describe ourselves and our work with words and phrases that are meaningful to those in our fields but meaningless to anyone outside of our immediate sphere. For example, many professionals use acronyms that have very specific, clear and defined meanings in their industries but are unintelligible to the rest of us.

I have coached individuals in the pharmaceutical industry, and it seems that people in that industry could form complete sentences with only acronyms! At first, I needed a translator in order to keep up. My clients were so familiar and comfortable with the acronyms they didn't even recognize they were speaking in a language others outside of their industry could not understand.

Other professionals fall into this jargon trap too. Let's take Alex, a lawyer, as an example. Imagine that Alex meets Kerry at a fundraising event for a local non-profit in which they're both involved. When Kerry asks Alex what he does for a living, Alex says that he is a securities litigator. This may make perfect sense to Kerry if she is also a lawyer or someone involved in highly sophisticated business transactions. However, "securities litigator" is not a phrase with which everyone is familiar. If Kerry is in a completely different field or industry, she may be desperately trying to figure out if a litigator is kin to an alligator or is some other kind of animal. It is a term she won't know, and she may not want to ask for more information for fear of exposing her ignorance and feeling embarrassed.

Similarly, a doctor might refer to herself by her medical specialty. Elizabeth is a highly trained doctor with a clearly defined area of practice. When asked what she does for a living, she typically states her specialty: "I am a geriatric neuroendocrinologist." To those who practice medicine, are in the medical field or have been a patient of Elizabeth's, geriatric neuroendocrinology is a known term. However, when Elizabeth states her specialty to anyone outside those spheres, she is often met with blank stares. If someone is bold enough to ask her to explain what that means, she will typically say that she focuses on the interaction between the nervous system and the endocrine system in older patients. For some this is enough, but for others she could explain even further ("I specialize in the interaction between the glands and the brain in seniors") so that everyone she encounters can get a clear picture of what she does and who her patients are likely to be.

We all need to think carefully about how we explain what we do depending upon our audience. Always ask yourself: Who am I talking with? Who is my audience? Where am I? What's my context?

The more you know about the person to whom you are speaking, the amount of time you have to tell you story, and the context in which you are telling it, the more likely it is that your efforts will hit their mark.

The other reason I recommend preparation is that when you first meet someone or start a self-promotion conversation, you have at most about 20 seconds to grab that person's attention. As I mentioned earlier, when I work with groups, I have them pair up and test out their self-promotion introductions. I give them 20 seconds and then ask them if the time seemed long or short. Universally, I get feedback that 20 seconds felt extremely short. The time goes by very quickly. Since we're not accustomed to sharing such short sound bites about ourselves, we have to prepare to maximize the time. If you're well prepared and you think about what you will say in those initial 20 seconds, you will have established your credibility and created enough curiosity to keep the conversation going.

I also want to take a moment to address other types of communication. We often have self-promotion opportunities in cyberspace and via phone, in addition to face-to-face. As with in-person conversations, you want to be prepared when you call someone on the phone. How will you describe yourself and what you do, particularly if you get their voicemail?

Remember that context is important and voicemail messages are another time when less is more. You need to be prepared to be clear, succinct and effective in promoting yourself by phone or voicemail.

Similarly, it is important to think of context and prepare accordingly when you have an opportunity to self-promote via email or online. Your email messages and even your signature block are self-promotion opportunities. Your LinkedIn profile and website bio are also venues for you to tell your story. There are many wonderful books about online presence and marketing, so I won't delve further into that subject here. Suffice it to say you need to prepare fully so that your story is consistent across all of these media and consider your audience as you choose your words.

In summary, prepare, prepare, prepare.

5. **Effective self-promoters believe that confidence and comfort go hand-in-hand.**

Those who have mastered the art of self-promotion come across confidently when telling their stories. They understand that their confidence leads to comfort for their audience. When we've thought ahead about the purpose, the audience and the context, we have more confidence delivering the message.

When we are confident telling our stories, our listeners are more comfortable, and the self-promotion is more effective. If the speaker is not confident, it makes the listener think — "Gee, if he's not confident and comfortable saying this, how can I be confident and comfortable with him?"

Josh is a great example of the importance of communicating your story confidently. Josh is a corporate marketing veteran. Over the years, he has held positions with several well-known consumer products companies. When we met, he was a senior director with a company that is responsible for many household name brands, and he was interviewing for a VP position with another organization. He told me that he felt extremely confident in his abilities. He knew he could do the job. However, he was not feeling comfortable talking about himself and his work.

I pointed out to Josh that even if he was confident in his work and his abilities, if he was not confident and comfortable *talking* about them, that lack of confidence would undermine the impression others have of him. Together we worked on increasing his comfort and confidence through a series of interview role plays.

As Josh learned, practice leads to confidence. In fact, you may even want to script what you will say and practice your self-promotion scripts. Whether you create talking points or a full-blown self-promotion story, putting your thoughts on paper (or at least on a computer screen) can help you dissect what you want to say and identify any potential stumbling blocks.

Perhaps, like me, you don't speak the way you write. As a result, I often find myself writing out what I want to say and then revising considerably after I practice saying it out loud. The most eloquently written self-promotion piece is only effective if you feel confident and comfortable when those words come out of your mouth. Therefore, you may write out your script and then tweak or change it based on your own speaking style before beginning to practice and commit it to memory.

However you choose to work on your self-promotion story, remember that if you're confident in the telling, your listener will be comfortable hearing what you share.

6. Effective self-promoters believe in positivity.

Although I don't know you personally, I know that you have had many successes in the course of your career, and these successes will serve as the backbone of your self-promotion stories.

In addition, it is likely that there have been some things in your career that you would say were less than successful.

Perhaps you lost your job, lost a key account or didn't get a coveted promotion. I heard countless stories like these during the economic downturn around 2008-2010.

We have all experienced setbacks in our careers, and even from these hardships and missteps, it's typically possible to extract something positive. What relationship did you build or grow? What did you learn from the experience? What skill did you pick up while you were job hunting? We always have the choice to focus on the positive, and effective self-promoters know that positivity is a key to storytelling success.

Positivity also means avoiding comparisons. Always frame your self-promotion as "I have done this," "my team has accomplished this," "we have contributed this" or "I have led this." Do not frame your self-promotion as a comparison. Avoid phrases like "more than," "compared to" and "better than."

Comparisons can be perceived as ugly, boastful or crude. So, it is important that you avoid them. Self-promotion isn't about putting down someone else; it's not about comparing yourself or what you've done to what anyone else has done or not done. It is only about you. That's the reason it is called "SELF-promotion."

Effective self-promoters know that telling your story means focusing attention on the positive about you.

7. **Effective self-promoters believe in honesty.**

I always debate whether to talk about this when I speak to a group, and I thought long and hard about whether to cover it here. However, I know that if I don't write about it, I will be overlooking an important belief that you must hold to master the art of self-promotion. It would be a disservice to you in your own self-promotion journey. I also know that honesty is often underrated or overlooked in the dog-eat-dog career world.

I'm constantly amazed by the stories I hear of people who play fast and loose with the truth in promoting themselves. We've all read stories of people who got caught lying on their resumes. Similarly, we have all heard people stretch the truth when telling their stories. I could tell you lots of incredible stories about the ways in which people have stretched the truth when promoting themselves. Not only is it morally reprehensible but it is also relationally repugnant. Keep it real. Tell the truth.

For example, if you play an important role on a project team, highlight your role but make sure that it is clear that you are part of a team. Own 100% of the work you did, and play that up, but don't allow your self-promotion to mislead your listener into thinking that you reached the goal all by yourself.

This is a delicate balance. Certainly, you do not want to talk about a team effort as if it were all your doing. Similarly you don't want to talk about it as if it was *all* a team effort and you barely played a role. Remember earlier when we talked about humility? This is the perfect time to tap into your sense of humility as a balance while being careful to ensure that humility does not overtake your story.

Remember to take credit where credit is due. Fully own the part you played and nothing more.

Entrepreneurial Spirit

In the last section, we covered the seven core beliefs of masterful self-promoters. I shared with you the key things that the most effective self-promoters know.

Now, I want to add one more layer. As I've mentioned, I have been in business for myself for many years. I owned a law practice for years before launching Novateur Partners, my executive coaching and leadership development business, in 2002.

As an entrepreneur engaged in a service business, one of the things I have learned is that I'm marketing a product and that product is me. I have a brand and must always be attuned to marketing my brand (more on brand in Chapter Six).

As business management guru, Tom Peters once said, "Regardless of age, regardless of position, regardless of the business we happen to be in, all of us need to understand the importance of branding. We are CEOs of our own companies: Me Inc. To be in business today, our most important job is to be head marketer for the brand called You."[8]

This lesson applies to you too. Even if you're not an entrepreneur and never intend to become one, you are marketing the product of you. Every time you interview for a job, every time you pitch a prospective client, every time you tell your boss why you should be promoted, you are marketing yourself — and if you're not, you should be! You should be telling your story in order to effect a specific result in your career.

And, if you are going to be telling your story, don't you want to be able to do so in an engaging way? Don't you want to market the product of you most effectively? As the CEO of Me Inc., you are in charge of the marketing and advertising campaign for Brand You.

Consider this scenario. Let's assume we work in an advertising agency and we represent a car company. Now assume we are trying to come up with a way to promote our client's latest model. We're all seated around a big conference table having a spirited discussion about the assets of this particular model of car and what makes it attractive to a prospective purchaser.

We turn our collective attention to the most effective method of ensuring that the car buying public knows about this car's assets. How do we let people know how great this car is? What will most effectively showcase this car?

In our discussion, we narrow our ideas down to two options. Option One is to take out an ad showing car buyers a specification sheet that details all of the features of this car. Perhaps this is an ideal way to let car buyers know about this terrific model. After all, it tells prospective buyers *everything* they could ever want to know about the car — standard features, gas mileage, number of seats, horsepower, available upgrades, dimensions, weight … you name it. This car has a lot to offer, and any prospective buyer would know it if he read the specification sheet.

Certainly it is important to know all of the features of a car before you purchase the car. We can all agree that at some point in the car buying process, it's good to know about the car's airbags and about its emergency braking system. We also know this is not what initially attracts the typical car buyer.

Back at the table in the ad agency, we consider Option Two. We could produce a full-color commercial showing the car on the road. The car in our ad would be a sexy red color.

We would set it against the backdrop of a beautiful two-lane road in a lush, green mountain setting and film it in a way that highlights the images of motion and speed. This commercial would show the car in action.

As we weigh our options, it becomes clear that Option Two is a more effective way to promote this car. Car buyers are initially attracted by the image and the aesthetics of the vehicle. Prospective buyers want to see how the car looks on the road, get a feel for how it handles and imagine how pleasant it might be to drive. The full-color commercial does not tell the prospective buyer everything she needs to know in order to buy the car, but it does establish initial credibility and create enough curiosity for her to head down to her local dealership or hop online to learn more.

Our ad agency chooses Option Two to promote the car.

How does this story apply to you as you promote yourself? These options for the car commercial mimic the options you have when promoting yourself. You could tell your target audience everything there is to know about you by, in effect, reading your resume. Or, you could simply touch on the highlights and begin to create the impression you want your target audience to have.

Remember that more is not always better when self-promoting. Said another way, less *is* more.

Just as the specification sheet in Option One was overkill when we were thinking about how to best promote the car, telling your entire life story, including every award you've won since kindergarten, is overkill in the context of self-promotion. You want to be selective. You want to establish a baseline of credibility and create just enough curiosity for the conversation to continue.

> Including every award you've won since kindergarten is overkill in the context of self-promotion.

When I see the red car in the commercial driving down the road, I think, "Wow, I like what I see. I want to know more." I can then ask questions, conduct research and find out about all of the car's standard features and available options. Similarly, when you're self-promoting, you want people to become interested in learning more about you, your strengths and your work. You should initially share enough to paint the picture in broad strokes. You can fill in the details later. You don't need to share everything up front.

Option Two — the full color commercial we chose for the car — is available to each of us as we consider our own self-promotion. In fact, you can — and should — become your own full-color, dynamic commercial for yourself. Option Two works because if you've begun the self-promotion process effectively, you have established your credibility and created a sufficient amount of curiosity to keep the conversation going.

Just as in the car commercial, it's critically important to share the most dynamic presentation of yourself so that your target audience is curious enough to want to know more. Through your self-promotion stories, you can embody a commercial for Me Inc. and its core brand — You.

To Know

- Self-promotion masters share seven core beliefs about themselves and their stories: (i) that telling their stories will transform their careers, (ii) in being sincere and authentic, (iii) in telling not selling, (iv) that preparation is critical, (v) that confidence and comfort go hand-in-hand, (vi) in focusing on the positive and (vii) in always being honest.

- Even if you're not an entrepreneur in the traditional sense, you have a product to commercialize and your product is you.

To Explore

- ❑ How many of the seven core beliefs of the masters do I hold?
- ❑ Where am I holding back?
- ❑ How can I better embody a full-color, dynamic commercial for myself?

Chapter Six

Reflect on It

Now that we have fully explored the beliefs you need to hold to master the art of self-promotion, let's take a look at what your self-promotion stories should include. After all, the story is only as good as its content.

How do you know what to promote about yourself? How can you best establish your credibility? What about you and what you do will create curiosity? What are the key components of your self-promotion story and what are the menu items from which you can pick and choose when crafting that story? To answer these questions, you have to begin to think about who you are and what you have to offer. What is it that sets you apart from someone else?

Although I may not know you personally, I feel secure in saying that you are not the only one who does whatever it is that you do. In fact, there are plenty of other people out there who do what you do.

There are countless marketing managers, CPAs, corporate lawyers, software developers, financial planners and project managers. But, you are the only *you* who does what you do. You have a unique set of strengths, accomplishments, passions and experiences that will increase the likelihood that people will want to want to hire you, promote you and bring you their best opportunities. You have a unique brand.

To know what your unique strengths, accomplishments, passions and experiences are, you will need to think about each of those things. You will need to carefully consider your brand. This means that you will need to engage in self-reflection.

Most of us are not self-reflection pros. We don't typically spend a lot of time engaged in introspective thinking. The world we live in is very action-oriented and our days generally don't include a lot of extra time for deep thinking.

You may be the exception to that rule and be very self-aware. Perhaps you devote time on an ongoing basis to self-reflection. Perhaps you regularly catalog your strengths, accomplishments, passions and experiences. Perhaps you've spent time defining your brand. However, chances are if you are reading this book you do not consistently engage in these activities. If you are going to master the art of self-promotion, you will need to set aside time regularly to engage in self-reflection.

The next several sections are going to help guide you as you begin the process of self-reflection. I am going to introduce several important concepts and then ask you the key questions that will help you mine for the material to include in your self-promotion stories. The information is inside you; we must simply unearth it. We must excavate the pieces of information that will form the backbone of your self-promotion story and give you the components you will need to build the most effective self-promotion piece for every audience and context.

Strengths

The best place to start the self-reflection process is with taking stock of your strengths. What are your unique talents? Where do you shine? Gallup, Inc., the global performance management consulting giant and publisher of a number of books on related subjects, defines a strength as "the ability to consistently provide near-perfect performance in a specific activity."[9]

You have a unique basket of talents and skills that define you. So, while others may share some of your strengths, you have an individualized combination of strengths that express themselves in a way that is particular to you. As Mr. Rogers used to sing on his show, "You are the only one like you."[10]

However, we often devalue our strengths. My executive coaching clients frequently tell me about something they think might be a strength but then backtrack by saying, "… but isn't everybody good at that?" My answer is an emphatic "No!" We each have areas of strength, and we need to own those.

What else keeps you from recognizing your strengths? Perhaps you can't recognize your strengths because you remember the times when you did not shine or when that strength did not come through. If I allow myself to think that being responsive is one of my strengths, I will quickly remember an example of a time when I did not respond quickly enough and it came back to bite me. We all have to move past the idea of perfection in order to recognize and catalog our very human strengths.

It's interesting to note that the mental muscles needed to master the art of self-promotion are closely related to the mental muscles required to graciously accept a compliment.

What do you say when someone compliments you? When I ask audiences or clients this question, the first answer I get is, "I say thank you." When I probe further, however, I hear things like, "I brush it off," "I minimize it" or "I deflect it."

Very often rather than graciously accepting the compliment someone gives us, we, in effect, return it to its sender.

We are very good at brushing off the compliment, minimizing it or deflecting it, all of which negate the compliment we were given. We say things like, "And you look nice as well." "Oh, this old thing?" Or, "It was nothing. We all pitched in. I really didn't do much at all." Women are especially talented when it comes to returning compliments to the sender.

Where does this tendency come from? Our discomfort with compliments likely originates in a false sense that simply accepting a compliment is not socially acceptable. Can you begin to see the similarities between compliments and self-promotion?

Therefore, as I said, in order to become more effective as a self-promoter, you must hone your skill of accepting compliments. How? Begin to simply accept a compliment with two words: "Thank you." After that, stop. Zip it. Say nothing else. Ignore that desire you may have to brush it off, minimize it or deflect it. Simply accept the compliment as given. Allow yourself to fully hear and take in what the other person has said, and then thank them. Accepting compliments will build your base of confidence and comfort, two essentials for mastering the art of self-promotion. Furthermore, this practice will help you begin to build the mental muscles you need to own your strengths.

Now, let's get back to your strengths. Think for a moment about the strengths you possess. What are five things you do particularly well, things you think are talents of yours?

When I ask clients and audiences whether they find this question difficult or easy to answer, I get a variety of responses. For a minority of people I work with, this question is easy to answer. Those few have a good handle on their top strengths and can quickly call them to mind. For the majority, however, this is a tough question to answer. Most of us find it hard to think of five things we do well. In fact, many people tell me that it is easier to come up with weaknesses than to catalog strengths.

If you struggled to come up with five strengths, here are a few ways to make the process a bit easier. First, consider the traits for which you are most frequently complimented. These compliments hold clues about your strengths. Pay attention to compliments and begin keeping a compliment log so you will be able to remember what people say are your strengths.

You may also want to take an assessment to help you figure out where some of your strength lie. The book *StrengthsFinder 2.0* by Tom Rath offers an assessment you can take online to discover your strengths. It also provides a wonderful explanation of each of the strengths it ranks so that you can begin to consider your strengths and how they show up for you.

Another tip for this exercise is to use the phrase "At my best, I am…" in order to mine for strengths. This helps silence that voice inside your head that reminds you of the times you did not show that strength or use that talent to its fullest. Remember, Gallup says a strength is "the ability to consistently provide *near-perfect* performance in a specific activity." It is about "near-perfect performance" and how you show up at your best, not about showcasing that strength perfectly, 100% of the time.

If you engage me as your executive coach, I will ask you to come up with not five, but 10, strengths. If you enjoy a challenge and want to earn extra credit as you work through this book, come up with five more strengths you possess. What are five additional areas in which you shine?

Simply naming your strengths can be a powerful exercise in building your confidence and providing the backbone of your self-promotion story. It is critically important that you know and own your strengths. Imagine how helpful it will be to have those strengths top of mind when you are interviewing, seeking a promotion or business building. And, there's more.

As writer, pastor and speaker Andy Stanley says, our "fully exploited strengths will always be more valuable to any organization than our marginally improved weaknesses."[11] Put in even simpler terms, our strengths are always our strong suit.

Therefore, whether or not you believe in focusing on improving your areas of weakness, you must always be aware of and fully leverage your strengths. In fact, identifying your strengths and being able to speak comfortably and confidently about them will be a tremendous asset to you throughout your career. You and your organization will reap the greatest benefit when you are leveraging your strengths.

You and your organization will reap the greatest benefit when you are leveraging your strengths.

As we bring this back to self-promotion and consider how to incorporate your strengths into your story, there is a second step. For each of the strengths you identify, I want you to think of an example or story that illustrates it. I think of these examples as "mini-movies."

I'm a visual person, and it's powerful for me to have a scenario I can visualize when I think of one of my strengths. By cataloging an example or story for each of my identified strengths, I am easily able to replay that example or story in my head each time I think of that particular strength.

As I already noted, these stories or examples are critically important because many people may self-identify as having a particular strength. However, that strength plays out differently for each person. The words we use to describe a strength we believe we possess — for example, reliable, hardworking, responsive and strategic — are often overused. As a result, those words can become fairly meaningless, unless we attach an illustration or a story to make that strength come alive.

What does being responsive really mean in the context in which you work? How has being responsive made a difference for your company or the clients you serve? Think of a time when your responsiveness made a difference.

Being able to tell a story or share an example of how your strength looks in action and the benefit your organization and clients have received as a result is a very powerful self-promotion tool. Once again, I am reminded of the importance of preparation. Considering these stories in advance will make it easy and seamless for you to call them to mind whenever you need them.

If you spend the time preparing, these mini-movies will be stored and cataloged in your head so that you can easily call them up in any situation. We have all had that "deer in the headlights" moment in which we need an example of a strength, but we can't think of a thing. Imagine the ease and confidence that will come from having these mini-movies ready when you have an opportunity to tell your story.

Let's take Heather as an example. Heather had been with the same technology company for most of her career and had moved up through the organization without ever having to formally interview for her next role. When the company undertook a massive reorganization, these changes signaled to Heather that it was time for her to leave.

She began job hunting, but given the number of years she had been out of the market, her comfort level was low. When she and I began working together, she recounted the story of an interview she had "bombed." She said she had awkwardly stalled for time when her interviewer asked her to describe a time when she leveraged one of her strengths for the benefit of a client. She knew that her strengths had benefitted clients immensely during her career, but in that moment, she couldn't think of a single example. She fumbled with her answer, her confidence dipped and the opportunity was lost.

In addition to suggesting that Heather catalog her strengths and come up with mini-movies to illustrate them, I suggested to her (and I suggest to you) that you play your mini-movies through in your mind on a regular basis. The more you review these examples and stories, the more you'll own them.

They will come alive for you, which will lead to increased comfort and confidence when it's time for you to share them with someone else. Your strengths form the foundation of your self-promotion efforts.

Accomplishments

As you spend time in self-reflection it is also important to consider and catalog your accomplishments. Simply because you are reading this book, I know you're a highly accomplished person. You have achieved a great deal in the course of your life to date.

One of the downsides of being a high achiever is that although we accomplish things all the time, we don't often recognize our day-to-day accomplishments; we only recognize our most significant accomplishments. Sure, we may recognize that graduating from college or getting an advanced degree is an accomplishment. We may note that landing a sought-after new job, getting a promotion or bringing in a big client is an accomplishment. However, when an accomplishment does not rise to our self-set high level, we tend to simply gloss over it and check the box. Yep, did that…what's next? We fail to appreciate what we've done and what it took to do it.

One of my clients, Rick, told me about his performance in an increasingly difficult role that included essentially doing the jobs of three people, "That's not really an accomplishment to me. That's just the nature of my job right now." Even when they are making great strides, I also hear clients say, "Well, of course I did that, doesn't everyone in my field do that?" We don't often recognize our own accomplishments. We take them for granted.

Among the many dangers of taking our accomplishments for granted is that if we're not aware of what we are accomplishing, we can't make anyone else aware. We must consciously note the things that we've done in the past in order to effectively tell someone else what we can do for them going forward. We need to know our own accomplishments so that we can share them when pitching a new client, seeking a promotion or interviewing for a job.

Interviewers, prospective clients and company leaders want to hear the stories of what you've accomplished. They want and need to know what you have done so they can gauge what you can do going forward. Do you have what it takes to perform in that sought-after job, take on the more senior role or serve that big, new client?

As you read this, chances are you're already thinking about your accomplishments. Or, if you're like some of my clients, perhaps you are thinking that you have not accomplished much.

Either way, I want you to thoughtfully consider what you have accomplished in the last year. What have you done, personally or professionally, in the last 12 months that you can be proud of? What are the projects you have completed? What tasks have you marked off your list? What have you achieved?

As you consider your accomplishments, remind yourself that no accomplishment is too small to be considered. After all, there was a time when tying your shoes was an accomplishment. Every accomplishment we make serves as a stepping stone as we move toward our next goal, so don't underestimate the importance of what you have achieved. In fact, smaller accomplishments along the way are often critical milestones without which we could never accomplish our big, audacious goals.

Now that you have considered some of your more notable accomplishments over the last year, let's delve a bit deeper into this topic. When I work with groups, at this point, I ask the audience members to pair up with someone sitting close to them and to each share one of their accomplishments. I tell the assembled group that there are three rules for this sharing game:

Rule # 1 Don't compare your accomplishments with those of others.

Whether you are sharing an accomplishment or listening to your partner's, don't make comparisons between your accomplishment and theirs. We naturally tend to compare, and these comparisons generally end up with judgments — of ourselves, our accomplishments or of the other person. Avoid comparisons in order to stay away from that quagmire.

Rule # 2 Own your accomplishments fully.

When you are sharing your accomplishment, avoid qualifying it. For example, if you lost 10 pounds in the last year, say it loudly and proudly — "I lost 10 pounds!" rather than saying "I did not lose as much as I had hoped, but I lost 10 pounds." Feel the difference?

Rule # 3 Enjoy the moment.

After you've listened to your partner's accomplishment, congratulate her. This is an appropriate time to ask a question to find out more about the accomplishment if it interests you but not to add your accomplishment to hers or to try to one-up her. Additionally, soak up the acknowledgement that comes from being congratulated on a hard-won accomplishment.

These three rules of the road are applicable whether you are sharing an accomplishment in one of my workshops or if you are sharing an accomplishment in a real-life self-promotion moment.

Given that you're reading this book rather than participating in one of my workshops (although if you haven't been to one of my workshops, I hope that someday you will), you may think you can't participate in the accomplishment game. Ah, but you can! I suggest that you find someone — a coach, a mentor, a peer or a friend — and share one of your accomplishments with that person. You should also ask your chosen partner to prepare an accomplishment he can share so you can both take a turn.

What is it like to hear someone else's accomplishment? How does it feel to share an accomplishment? When I ask these questions in groups, I get a variety of answers, but overall I hear that it's a good experience. Contrary to what we may have been taught, it feels good to share something good. It is not uncomfortable and is actually a motivating experience for you *and* your listener.

A few notes from the many times I have asked groups to participate in this exercise: The first is about how we can sometimes subtly undermine ourselves when sharing an accomplishment. The tone of voice you use when sharing makes a difference.

Often when we share an accomplishment, we sound overly modest or nearly ashamed to be sharing. In that case, we do not fully own the accomplishment. When we do not fully own an accomplishment, our listener can hear it. It undermines our credibility and makes our storytelling far less effective. Remember that if you are confident, your listener will be more comfortable, which will lead to more effective self-promotion.

Second, allow your excitement to come through when you share your accomplishment. After all, it's likely that what you are sharing involved hard work, perseverance, diligence and a whole host of other qualities that you had to summon or develop. It was exciting when you achieved it, and it should be exciting sharing that achievement with someone else. Allow those emotions to permeate your words and your tone as you speak. This is great practice for bringing passion to your self-promotion efforts.

Third, know that people enjoy and benefit from hearing the accomplishments of others. You may feel that your audience will be bored and disinterested, but in reality, it is energizing to hear what someone else has accomplished. We're motivated and inspired by the accomplishments of others. If that were not the case, there would not be so many motivational speakers who earn handsome fees simply talking about what they've accomplished.

We are fueled to accomplish more when we hear what others have achieved.

> **We're motivated and inspired by the accomplishments of others.**

When I am working with a group, I up the ante after the pairs exchange accomplishments by asking if anyone has an accomplishment they'd like to share with the whole group. I remind them that they are in a *self-promotion* workshop. When I make this invitation, an interesting thing happens. Typically, one or two people immediately jump at the chance to share with the group, while everyone else sits silently.

What makes most of the group sit silently and look away when I make this invitation? All they have to do is stand up, introduce themselves and share one accomplishment. It doesn't get any easier than that. The workshop is a safe venue with a group of people who are all present because they want to master the art of self-promotion. It is the perfect environment in which to practice owning accomplishments by sharing with the whole group. And yet, very few people take me up on my invitation.

The reason why so few people are willing to share their accomplishments is simple. Self-promotion is outside of many people's comfort zones. As I've said, it is not something we are accustomed to doing and we hold negative mindsets about it. All of that leads to reluctance to share.

You can call this reluctance fear or you can chalk it up to the little voice inside your head. We all know that voice. It is the voice that says, "Sharing an accomplishment would be really uncomfortable. Everyone would be paying attention to me and judging me." Or perhaps, "I don't know if my accomplishment is really big enough or important enough to warrant sharing it with others." Or perhaps your inner voice says something like, "Don't say anything. You know you really don't like talking about yourself."

Whatever that voice inside your head says, in his book, *Taming Your Gremlin*, Rick Carson notes that the most important first step is to simply listen. Notice that the voice is there and hear what it is saying. The voice is not bad or wrong, it simply is part of being human. We all grapple with inner critical voices or "gremlins," as Carson calls them.

No matter how accomplished you become, those inner critical voices don't go away. What they're saying may change, but they do not leave us. The key is to notice and begin learning to move beyond what they tell you. We can learn to listen to that voice less and train ourselves to say, "Thanks for sharing that sentiment, but I'm still going to go ahead and talk about my accomplishments, so get over it!"

We can move past the inner critical voice, or at least turn down the volume, so we can hear what is really true for us in any given moment.

Whatever your inner critical voice is telling you about sharing an accomplishment with others is what you must overcome in order to be a more effective self-promoter. That message is your personal challenge when it comes to self-promotion; it's the thing that's keeping you from telling your story. It's your own personal road block, the barrier you need to get past in order to master the art of self-promotion. It's a previously hidden mindset that has now come to light. So, whatever that voice is saying, be sure you're listening so you can disarm it.

I'm often asked if this reluctance to share an accomplishment is different for men than it is for women. Do men have an easier time turning down the noise and embracing their accomplishments? In my coaching work, I have seen both men and women struggle with this, and when I present workshops, an equal number of men and women will typically stand up to share an accomplishment with the whole group. Based on that non-scientific data, I would say that this reluctance is relatively consistent across both genders.

If self-promotion were easy (for men or women), I would not have needed to write this book and you would not be taking your precious time to read it. Mastering the art of self-promotion is not easy for most people – male or female.

Regardless of your gender, your job is to overcome your personal internal roadblocks and to take advantage of opportunities to self-promote whenever they arise. Tell yourself that it may be uncomfortable at first but that the payoff makes it worthwhile. With repeated practice, your self-promotion muscle, like any other muscle, will strengthen. Sharing your accomplishments will become easier and more comfortable.

Carol is a great example of that principle. I spoke about self-promotion at a women's networking group several years ago. At the time, Carol was incoming president of the organization. The next year, when she was in her new role, she engaged me as her coach. Carol is very accomplished in her career, dedicated to several community and business organizations and was never comfortable sharing her achievements. As I coached her, we began to discuss self-promotion and how valuable it can be when done effectively.

While Carol agreed that self-promotion is important, she remained reluctant to promote herself, tell her story or share any of her accomplishments. It was only when she realized that her position as president of the networking group made her a role model for other women that she began to shift her mindset. She then understood that self-promotion was something she needed to do not only for herself but also for the women she was leading.

She received a promotion that year and she decided to share that big accomplishment with the networking group when she was at the podium at the next luncheon meeting. From there, she invited others to share accomplishments through the group's newsletter, online and at the luncheons. She worked to create a culture in which everyone felt empowered to self-promote and tell their stories.

Although she was initially uncomfortable, during this process Carol was able to become confident about promoting herself, telling her story and ensuring that others knew who she was and what she had accomplished. In addition to acting as a terrific role model for the other members, Carol also built her storytelling muscle. She mastered the art of self-promotion.

Carol's story is a great example of sharing an accomplishment at the time it happens, but what about all those accomplishments we make and then forget about? Given that it's important to be aware of your accomplishments and to be able to recount them, I suggest keeping an accomplishment log.

By tallying your accomplishments, you become more aware of what you're doing, and that awareness helps fuel more accomplishment. Cataloging accomplishments can actually serve as rocket fuel to help you accomplish even more. Accomplishment feeds more accomplishment. It creates momentum.

Accomplishment feeds more accomplishment. It creates momentum.

Keeping up with your accomplishments weekly, or even daily, gives you more content for your stories which in turn makes you a more effective self-promoter.

Although we have established that you should be promoting yourself all the time, if you're like most people, your default is to only promote yourself at performance review time (if, in fact, you have a performance review). Often a significant amount of time passes between reviews. It could be as much as six months or a year, and I don't know about you, but if you ask me what I've accomplished in the last year, without some sort of list or log, I will be hard pressed to remember everything. As time passes, accomplishments fade from our memories.

By cataloging your accomplishments as they happen, you stop that fade. An accomplishment log will help you to be more prepared to promote yourself when the opportunity arises because your accomplishments will be fresh in your mind. In addition, when you have a big opportunity — like the opportunity to pitch yourself for a promotion, or for a new job or to a new client — those accomplishments will be right there in your log, readily accessible, so it will be easy to recall and talk about what you've done and how you've done it. This log, along with the compliment log I mentioned in the prior section, will serve as an excellent resource for your self-promotion efforts. Once cataloged, your accomplishments can take a starring role in your story.

Passion

As you reflect on who you are and what you've done, it is also important to identify what you love about your work. What are you passionate about in what you do? When we're passionate about our work, it comes across when we speak. It enrolls our audience, and they want to hear more. Passion is engaging. It naturally helps you tell your story in a way that makes people sit up and take notice.

As an aside, when I asked, "What are you passionate about in your work?" if you thought "nothing," then you need to engage in a different kind of conversation. Several of the coaches at Novateur Partners specialize in working with people who want to explore career transition, and perhaps that is the next step in transforming your career. If so, let us know. It is an important conversation to have, but it is a different conversation from the one we're having in this book. For now, let's assume that there is something you love (or at least like) about what you do.

To fully master the art of self-promotion, you must know why you find joy in what you are doing, where your passion lies in your work and what you love about your field. What do you bring to your clients? What is it that excites you about what you do? Aside from the paycheck, what is it that keeps you doing what you do? What are you passionate about in the work that you do? Why did you choose the field in which you work, the organization you work for, the kind of clients that you represent and the product you market?

When you answer these questions and hone in on your passion, your self-promotion becomes easier and more natural. We already discussed that tapping your love for what you do will go a long way to ensuring you are able to authentically self-promote. Remember that enthusiasm is contagious. When you are able to exude passion, people will naturally want to work with you, hire you, promote you and team up with you.

Keep in mind that passion doesn't look the same on everybody. Passion can look animated and bubbly. It can also show up in the form of depth of knowledge. Really deep interest in a subject can convey passion, just as enthusiasm and animation can. Show passion about your work in a way that is comfortable and natural for you.

For example, when I planned to move to another part of Atlanta, I began considering which real estate agent to work with. The decision was easy. I know an agent, Rita, who is truly passionate about her work. Her enthusiasm is contagious. She enjoys showing houses, she likes the negotiation process and she gets a real charge out of seeing people settle into their dream homes.

Rita engages in authentic self-promotion that centers around her love of her work and enrolls new clients with ease because of her passion. Rita's passion reveals itself in her animated and bubbly style.

On a related note, not long ago, I needed to purchase a new mattress. I see a mattress as a means of getting a good night's sleep and not much more. I don't know much about mattresses and can't muster a lot of my own passion around making such a purchase. Knowing this was a purchase I had to make, I set out to visit several mattress stores to check out different options and pricing. Admittedly as I went into the first store, I was thinking that it was going to be an unpleasant buying experience. I envisioned having to listen to sales pitches about mattresses and spending hours and hours on this mundane task.

All that would have been true had I not encountered Travis, the salesperson at the first mattress store I visited. Travis was truly passionate about mattresses. Although of course he wanted to sell me a mattress, his passion focused on mattresses themselves — how they're constructed, the different types and the various ways that people sleep depending upon what they find comfortable. He was deeply knowledgeable about mattresses.

When I thought I'd found one I really liked, he encouraged me to try out several other, very diverse models as well and explained their differences in detail.

His passion was very engaging, and because he was passionate about his work, I wanted to give him my business. Travis' passion expressed itself through his depth of knowledge.

I've just given you two examples, one for someone promoting themselves in connection with a service (residential real estate) and the other with a product (mattresses). The formula is the same in any profession. We can all think about or remember a time when we've had the opportunity to work with someone who is truly passionate about what they do. It makes a huge difference. It engages and energizes people. It makes clients want to hire you. It inspires the people you work with to want to put you on the teams they lead. It helps you land the job you seek. We must understand and harness the power of passion if we are going to master the art of self-promotion.

Experiences

We all have unique life experiences, those interesting tidbits in our backgrounds that set us apart. Unearthing yours is important to your storytelling. Remember that one of the goals of your self-promotion efforts is to create curiosity. Recalling your unique life experiences and sharing them creates that curiosity in your audience.

Those experiences and stories make others want to ask questions and keep the conversation going. They allow people to connect with you and to begin to create a relationship with you.

It is axiomatic that people hire people. People promote people. Clients engage a particular person because they feel a connection, because they're able to begin to build some sort of relationship and rapport with the person. Creating connection and building relationship is critical, and there's no more effective way to do that than through sharing interesting experiences you've had.

Your inner critical voice may be piping up now, telling you that there is nothing all that interesting about your life experiences. It may be saying, "Who are you to think that people would find *that* interesting?" Often the things about ourselves that we take for granted are the very things that are most interesting to others. What is it about you that sets you apart from someone else who does the same kind of work that you do? What experiences are unique to you?

I worked with Larissa on her self-promotion story several years ago. She is a financial advisor who owns a planning firm. The firm focuses on financial planning for small business owners.

As we considered how she could be more effective in her self-promotion, we talked about what differentiates her from other people who do financial planning, and more specifically, what differentiates her from others who do financial planning for small business owners.

As Larissa began to think more deeply about how she got into her niche and why she's passionate about what she does, she was reminded of something: an interesting fact about herself and her background. Larissa is a fourth-generation entrepreneur. Four generations ago, her family owned and ran a general store, and in each subsequent generation, there has been an entrepreneur in the family.

Over the generations, Larissa's family faced the very same financial planning issues that her clients now face. They grappled with issues like succession planning, inheritance and taxes, just as Larissa's clients do. Not only is Larissa interested in and passionate about these issues, but she can also tell a personal story about how her family history is tied to her being in her field. Her experience is interesting, it's unusual and it sets her apart.

Larissa can tell the story of her ancestor's general store and the kinds of challenges he faced as a small business owner. That story and those of her other relatives who have run businesses tie together and make her self-promotion story more compelling. And, she herself is now a small business owner, so the pieces come together beautifully into a story that makes her self-promotion much more effective than it would be otherwise.

You may not believe that there's anything in your background that ties so neatly to your work, and perhaps there isn't something as clear and direct for you as there is for Larissa. However, when you consider your own experiences, the obstacles you've overcome and the adventures you've had, you will find the stories that will set you apart. These experiences are part of what make your self-promotion story more compelling.

As you think back over the course of your life and career, begin to draw a line from your past experiences to your current career goals. Although it isn't always a straight line, you'll likely begin to discern a general direction or some patterns that emerge. Those will form the baseline of your self-promotion stories in the same way that being a fourth-generation entrepreneur created Larissa's.

I drew this line for my own self-promotion story. Remember my role in *Annie Get Your Gun*? On the surface, my role in our fourth grade play would not seem to tie to my current career as an executive coach, speaker and workshop leader, but in fact, it does. My desire to be on stage (coupled with my lack of musical ability) ultimately led me in the direction of my current career.

That piece of my past is an experience that I can, and often do, weave into my self-promotion story.

When I conduct self-promotion workshops, at this juncture I ask everyone to jot down three unique experiences they have had in the course of their lives to-date. I then ask them to partner with someone and share one of those experiences. When they do, something amazing, but not surprising, always happens — they connect and engage with each other on a deeper, more personal level. The level of energy in the room rises, people smile, they laugh and everyone feels good.

By sharing our personal experiences, we create just enough vulnerability so that our listener begins to feel that they know us and can relate. Reflecting on your life experiences and seeing how they've influenced your career can help you begin to create more connection and curiosity while ensuring that your self-promotion is more effective.

Brand

As you reflect, your brand is the final piece of the puzzle that will help you tie all of these components (strengths, accomplishments, passion and experiences) together into a coherent self-promotion story. Last chapter, I introduced the concept of branding and the notion that we're all engaged in marketing our product — Brand You.

What is your brand? When I ask clients this question, I often get a blank stare in response. We all have a brand, whether we have consciously created it or whether it has evolved by default. You may know what your brand is (or think you know), or you may not have any insight into this question. Either way, let me begin by defining the term "brand" for you.

In the past, a brand was seen simply as the trademark for a product or service mark for a particular service. When I practiced trademark law, I often worked with the client's branding experts to help them protect their brand by registering a trademark.

However, in today's business environment, the brand name or trademark is only one component of brand. In fact, there are as many different definitions of brand as there are people interested in the topic. Author and branding expert Seth Godin defines brand as, "…the set of expectations, memories, stories and relationships that, taken together, account for a consumer's decision to choose one product or service over another."[12]

Jerry McLaughlin, who writes for Forbes.com, said, "Put simply, your 'brand' is what your prospect thinks of when he or she hears your brand name. It's everything the public thinks it knows about your name brand offering — both factual (e.g. It comes in a robin's-egg-blue box.) and emotional (e.g. It's romantic.)" [13]

As you can see, these definitions are designed to apply best to a product or service offering, rather than to a personal brand, but the same logic applies to us as individuals.

As you read these definitions, you probably noted that there's a clear theme. Brand is in the eye of the beholder. Brand relies on what someone thinks about the product, service or person in question. As David McNally and Karl D. Speak said in *Be Your Own Brand*, "Your brand is a perception or emotion, maintained by somebody other than you, that describes the total experience of having a relationship with you."[14]

What do people think of when they hear your name? If I interviewed the people who are most influential to your career, what would you want them to say about you? What would they actually say about you? And, most importantly, are your answers to these last two questions the same? Is there alignment between what you want your brand to be and the brand you have already established? You have a brand already, whether you know what it is or not. People have formed perceptions of you, what you offer and how you do what you do.

Let's look at this principle another way. If pressed, you could probably tell me what you want your brand to be. You have an idea of what you want to stand for and how you want to be perceived. Those ideas form your brand promise.

Your brand arises from how you deliver on the promises you make.

Your brand arises from how you deliver on the promises you make. Sounds simple, right? Let's consider the concept in more detail though.

Let's say that you've developed a new type of toothpaste, and you decide that the toothpaste's brand promise will be "whiter teeth in 30 days." That, then, is the promise you make in your advertising campaign. "Whiter teeth in 30 days" will, in fact, become the toothpaste's brand if, and only if, people who use the toothpaste find that their teeth become whiter within 30 days of switching to your toothpaste. If their teeth do not become whiter, then "whiter teeth in 30 days" will not be your toothpaste's brand. Instead, it will be an empty promise on which the toothpaste fails to deliver.

The opposite can also be true. Let's say a business consultant starts his business without making an explicit brand promise. He doesn't articulate a brand, but he knows how he wants to do business. He returns calls promptly, follows through on commitments and delivers a quality service to his clients. Over time, a brand gets established for him and his business because he has delivered responsiveness, follow through and quality. Those perceptions define and become his brand.

I would argue that now he could — and should — articulate these into a formal brand promise, the components of which will become an important part of how he promotes himself and his business.

Now that we've clarified the definition of brand, what is yours? What are the key adjectives you would want someone to use when describing you? Are those the same adjectives that someone would use now? If there's a disconnect between the adjectives you *want* someone to use to describe you (your brand promise) and the adjectives people would *currently* use, you are not creating a strong brand. In this case, you need to take steps to align people's perceptions with your desired brand.

Getting clarity on your brand and considering how well you are fulfilling your brand promise can help you align your actions with your desired brand more effectively. This clarity can also help you craft your self-promotion story so that it reinforces the brand you want to create. As business management expert Tom Peters said, "You're every bit as much a brand as Nike, Coke, Pepsi, or The Body Shop."[15]

Take my brand for example. As an executive coach, keynote speaker and workshop leader, I want to be known as credible, experienced, wise, practical and in full possession of a sense of humor, especially about myself. As I developed my *Annie Get Your Gun* narrative, I worked to ensure that my story reinforced the qualities of my brand. With that clarity, I try to ensure that the work I do and the way I communicate are consistent with that brand so that I fulfill my brand promise each and every day.

Your self-promotion stories must not only be consistent with your brand, but they must be implementable and implemented regularly. In other words, it's not enough to have a good story; you must consistently and constantly tell it. That type of consistency — in your brand, your self-promotion story and your actions — will ensure that you are in the driver's seat of your own career.

To Know

- ☐ Your strengths, accomplishments, passion and experiences set you apart from the countless others who do what you do.
- ☐ You, your clients and your organization benefit most when you know and are leveraging your strengths.
- ☐ You accomplish things all the time. Knowing what you've achieved and what it took to achieve it will help you tell your story more effectively.
- ☐ Passion can reveal itself through enthusiasm and through deep knowledge.
- ☐ Your life experiences connect you to others and enrich your self-promotion.
- ☐ Your brand is what others think about you, the work you do and the way you do it.

To Explore

- ❑ Notice how you respond when someone pays you a compliment. Begin to practice accepting the compliment by saying, "Thank you" and nothing more.
- ❑ Keep a compliment log in which you note the compliments you receive.
- ❑ What are five strengths I possess? For extra credit, come up with 10.
- ❑ Catalog an example or story that illustrates each of your strengths. Replay these "mini-movies" frequently so they stay top of mind.
- ❑ What have I accomplished, personally and professionally, over the last 12 months?
- ❑ Find a buddy and share accomplishments. Notice how motivating the process is.
- ❑ Keep an ongoing accomplishment log so that your achievements are not forgotten.

- ❑ What excites me about my work, the clients I serve and the industry or field in which I work? How do I express my passion?
- ❑ What life experiences have I had that set me apart?
- ❑ What do people think of when they hear my name? What do I want them to think? Are my answers to these two questions aligned?

Chapter Seven

"Sanctioned" Self-Promotion

Throughout this book, I've repeatedly said that you must tell your self-promotion stories regularly. Over time you will be presented with numerous opportunities for self-promotion. Some of them will come out of the blue, like my airplane experience from Chapter Five. However, there are instances in which self-promotion is expected. There are certain circumstances in which you *must* be prepared to self-promote. While you should be ready to tell your story at any time, in any context and to any audience, there are certain contexts in which you know you need to be prepared to tell your story. Let's spend some time on those now.

The Performance Review

Most of my clients (even the ones who feel uncomfortable talking about their accomplishments in other settings) will admit that it's okay to self-promote during a performance review. And, although performance reviews are only the tip of the iceberg when it comes to times when it is appropriate to tell your story, they are critical self-promotion opportunities. A performance review is what I call a "sanctioned" time for self-promotion, so you simply must take full advantage of it.

> There are certain circumstances in which you *must* be prepared to self-promote.

Employers expect self-promotion during the performance review process. In fact, many companies ask employees to complete self-evaluations in preparation for a review. If your company requires this step, you are in luck. It is likely that they will provide you with a format and/or form to complete so you have a framework in which to tell your story.

When writing up your self-evaluation, be sure to state the facts in a clear, affirmative manner. Avoid adding qualifiers such as, "In my opinion," "I think," or "I believe" and simply state your accomplishments without backpedaling. This is your time to shine and to ensure that those with the power to influence your career path know what you've done and how you have done it.

Obviously promoting yourself at a performance review is made simpler if the company provides you with a form or format for telling your story. However, even if there is not a formal process in place for you to provide input, a performance review is the perfect opportunity to ensure that your organization knows what you do, how well you do it and how much value you add. Absent a framework, it still makes sense to write up your story so that you are adequately prepared for your review.

As I mentioned earlier, it's easy to think that your boss and those in leadership roles will already know all about you, but in reality, those reviewing you may not be the people closest to the work you do. In many companies and firms, your manager or boss won't even be in the room for your performance review. Those who are present may be several layers removed from having first-hand knowledge of you and your work-product.

Whether you're completing a form or simply preparing to be a powerful participant in your review, a review is an ideal time to revisit your strengths, accomplishments, passion, experiences and brand. What are the highlights of your last year? How do those stories point in the direction of advancement? What do you want the next step of your career to be?

As we discussed before, preparation is critical. You will want to prepare fully so that you can talk about yourself and your work confidently and comfortably.

In addition to being an opportunity for an evaluation of your work to date, performance reviews are a great venue for expressing where you want to go in the organization and why you are perfectly positioned to go there. Declare your intentions. Being clear about what you want in your career helps put your self-promotion efforts into context.

Let me give you an example. A client of mine, Susan, had achieved a great deal of success in her career and was enjoying her role as a director in a global hospitality company. She managed a team, had a lot of responsibility and was regularly challenged to learn. The next step for Susan would be a move into a VP-level role, and although she was open to the idea of such a move, she was not wedded to getting that role. In other words, she was feeling fulfilled in her career already so the move up to an officer position would be a "nice to have" but not a "got to have" promotion.

Susan knew that there was an opening at the VP-level and that she might be considered for the role. When I asked her if she wanted the new role, she said that given she was being considered for it, she would certainly be pleased to get it.

She and I both knew that her colleague, Oliver, was also in consideration for the role and that he had made a very clear statement of his interest, something Susan had never done.

I asked Susan how she would feel if Oliver got the role. She told me clearly that she was the better, more qualified candidate and that while she was happy in her current role, she would be disappointed and feel overlooked if Oliver was moved into the VP-level position. At that moment, Susan had an "ah-ha." If she was truly interested in the VP role, she had to make that intention clear and engage in some self-promotion. It was not enough for her to sit back and wait to be given the role based on her qualifications and contributions; she had to be sure that the right people knew that she was interested *and* qualified. She had to make her intentions known and back those intentions up with the success stories to prove her case.

Her next performance review was right around the corner, and Susan was ready. She prepared her case for promotion and was able to comfortably and confidently showcase her strengths and accomplishments. She passionately stated her interest in the VP role. She kept her brand in mind — committed, reliable, hard-working, eager to learn and responsive — and told stories that illustrated those qualities. Susan's bosses were impressed with her accomplishments, storytelling and obvious passion for growth within the company.

They unanimously agreed that she was the right person for the VP position and offered her the promotion.

Later, after she had settled into her new role, Susan reflected on the importance of having clearly stated her intentions. She knew that letting her company's leadership know that she wanted the role and focusing on telling her story with the promotion in mind ensured that she was offered the VP position. She used her performance review not only to look backward but also to proactively steer the direction of her career.

The Job Interview

Job interviews are another "sanctioned" self-promotion opportunity. When you're interviewing for a job, it's absolutely critical that you tell your story clearly, confidently and powerfully. You need to be able to engage your interviewers and let them know what separates you from the pack. Self-promotion is expected. In fact, if you don't self-promote when interviewing, I can promise you that you won't get the job.

I frequently work with people who are in career transition, voluntary or not. I always remind my clients that the interview process has two key components, two things that a prospective employer is looking for in an interview. The first is technical competency. Can you do the job?

Being clear about your strengths and accomplishments and being able to talk about them in a compelling way will help convince your interviewers that you have the chops to do the job.

If you have interviewed for a position recently, then you've probably encountered the behavioral interviewing technique. Behavioral interviewing is based on the premise that past performance is the best indicator of future behavior. As a result, interviewers who use this technique ask questions about situations you have experienced in the past so they can get a good read on how you would perform in the role they are seeking to fill.

As you can imagine, given this approach, if you can't relate your strengths and accomplishments to the interviewer — if you can't tell those stories — then she won't be able to accurately evaluate how well you will perform in the role you seek. Behavioral questions are the perfect opportunity for you to tell parts of your story and clearly show your prospective employer that you have the required competencies for the job.

The second thing that interviewers seek to determine during the interview process is whether they want to work with you. What would make the interviewer want to hire you as opposed to another candidate who also possesses the required technical competencies to do the job?

The *way* you tell your story is as important as having a clear and compelling story to tell.

Can your interviewer connect with you? Do you leave them thinking: "Yep. This is somebody I want on our team." "This is somebody I want to work with on a daily basis." "I'd be comfortable walking down the hall and having a conversation with this person." "This is someone I'd like to go have a beer with after work." You get the idea. In order to ensure that the answer to these questions is a resounding "Yes!" you must tell your story authentically and effectively.

Roy's story illustrates this perfectly. Roy had been working for his family's home building company for a number of years. When I met him, he had decided to leave that company and re-enter the job market. He had a great resume, was incredibly smart and technically competent. His knowledge was up-to-date and he could answer any substantive question his interviewers posed, but he was not getting any job offers. He was puzzled and disheartened.

I asked Roy some questions about the interview process. As we talked, he began to realize that he was completely focused on letting his interviewers know he could do the job rather than also focusing on building rapport. He realized that he needed to take a more integrated approach in his interviews, show more of his personality and focus on relationship as well as competence.

This subtle shift in mindset made all the difference in his interviewing success. In fact, shortly thereafter when he got an interview with his dream company, he focused on telling his story while building rapport, and he was offered the job.

Remember the Mindsets of the Masters in Chapter Five? In that chapter, I covered the beliefs you need to hold in order to master the art of self-promotion. When preparing for an interview, it's important to be sure that you make those fundamental mindset shifts. And, if you don't recall those beliefs, I suggest revisiting Chapter Five now.

Internal Brand Building

Although performance reviews and job interviews are the most common self-promotion opportunities — i.e. times when you are literally being asked to tell your story — there are many other times when self-promotion is both necessary and appropriate. Even if you have the job of your dreams and you want to stay there forever, if you're not letting people know what you're doing and how you're doing it, your company's leaders may not perceive your value in that role. You must self-promote to build and maintain your brand within the organization.

Let's take the example of Kevin. Kevin is a loan officer at a bank. The bank prizes strong relationships and community presence because those activities lead to the development of more business. For years, both because it was good for business and because he was passionate about the cause, Kevin had been deeply involved in a local non-profit organization. As a result of his dedication and hard work, he had recently been selected to the Board of the organization.

When the organization held a luncheon to celebrate having achieved a fundraising objective and to present a check to the community it supports, Kevin invited his boss and some of his colleagues. More than 300 local luminaries, business leaders and community members who benefitted from the organization's services comprised the capacity crowd. Kevin chaired the event and was selected to present the very large check to the foundation his organization was funding.

That day, when Kevin and his boss walked into the room, his boss looked around in awe. She noted the large number of people present and the high profile attendees. She saw the professionalism of the group and the level of respect Kevin had within the organization. She remarked to Kevin, "Wow! I didn't know how involved you were in this group. This is a big deal. You are really important!" And Kevin, sense of humor intact, responded, "Yes. I am really important. That's why I invited you!"

Sometimes self-promotion is not about the words you say but about being observed at your best. Kevin promoted himself best by inviting his boss to see him in the context of some of the great work he was doing. By seeing the scope of what Kevin had accomplished within the organization, his boss was able to see Kevin's passion, skills and abilities more clearly. Even more importantly, she was able to see Kevin as a leader.

Regardless of where you work, you need to do whatever you can to ensure that you're perceived as valuable to that organization. Remember, your brand exists whether you are working to create it or not. To create perceived value, you must consciously build your internal brand through self-promotion. You should constantly be telling your story so that people know what you've accomplished and why you are an asset to the business. For others to perceive your value, you must self-promote. After all, no one knows you — and your skills and accomplishments — better than you.

You should constantly be telling your story so that people know what you've accomplished and why you are an asset to the business.

Business Development

Self-promotion is also necessary and appropriate for anyone involved in business development. Business development is not only for those employed in traditional sales roles.

Today, it's a critical part of the job description for most professionals (CPAs, consultants, financial planners, executive coaches, real estate agents, insurance brokers) and anyone engaged in an entrepreneurial enterprise or a role that requires an ongoing stream of clients. For example, young lawyers are encouraged to spend the majority of their time developing their technical competency in the practice of law. However, for those working in a law firm, at some point in their career paths, the ability to develop business will become critical to their advancement and continued career success.

As I described in Chapter Five, when you meet someone new you have less than 20 seconds to establish your credibility with that person and create enough curiosity to ensure that the conversation continues. To be effective as a business developer, you must be prepared to tell your story succinctly and clearly. You must also take into account your audience and context. Whether you are circulating at a cocktail party, sitting at a table at a business event or hanging out at a neighborhood barbeque, you may have the opportunity for business development.

Years ago, a colleague, Laura Biering, and I developed the concept of Organic Networking. We believed (and still do) that you can develop business by being who you are and doing the things you enjoy. With that in mind, you can be engaged in business development anytime and all the time. To be most effective though, you must be prepared to tell your story.

Remember David from Chapter One? David is the CPA who works in a small firm. Business development is critical to his success at the firm, and when I met David, he told me that he frequently meets new people. He's active in his neighborhood and in his children's activities. He had many opportunities to build the relationships that would lead to business, but he wasn't telling his story. He was so afraid of being an over-promoter that he wasn't even letting his friends and neighbors know what he did for a living. Imagine trying to build a CPA practice and develop a client base when you are afraid to tell people what you do for a living!

The result was that he was not developing business even though he (and the partners at his firm) recognized that he had lots of potential client development opportunities through the people he naturally encountered. He was engaged in organic networking activities but wasn't capitalizing on the contacts he was making.

David was a tough nut to crack, but after several coaching appointments in which we explored his existing mindset and the opportunities he was missing, he decided to adopt a more empowering mindset about self-promotion and try it out.

Once he realized that the work he does really helps others, that realization gave him the confidence he needed to tell his story. He decided to begin letting people know what he did for a living and to tell a story or give input when accounting-related topics came up. He worked on a short statement he could easily and comfortably deliver when people asked him what he did for a living and practiced it so that it flowed easily. Then, he began sharing it.

What a difference! Rather than sheepishly saying, "I'm a CPA" when asked what he does for a living, David began embracing his role. He began confidently telling people that he helps businesses get a handle on their numbers so that they can do what they do best. He learned to powerfully respond to their questions, sharing just enough about who he is and what he does to establish his credibility and create curiosity so that conversations continue. Over time, and with continued practice, David found that telling his story, promoting himself and sharing more about his work could be gratifying. As he continued to network in his neighborhood and through his children's activities, he realized that he could comfortably and confidently develop business by being who he is and doing what he enjoys.

As David's example proves, it is never too late to start developing business, and you can tell your story in a way that is comfortable for you. The sooner you recognize the importance of self-promotion to your career, the better. The more effective you become at telling your story, the more you will be able to create transformation in your career.

To Know

- ❑ Although you need to be prepared to tell your story any time and all the time, there are certain scenarios in which self-promotion is an absolute must: (i) performance reviews, (ii) job interviews, (iii) internal brand building and (iv) business development.
- ❑ Performance reviews are an ideal time to talk about what you have done and where you want to go in the future.
- ❑ Job interviews are showcase opportunities for strengths, accomplishments and passion, and the way you tell your story is as important as what you share.
- ❑ Brand building within your organization requires that you constantly tell your story.
- ❑ Business development and networking require the ability to establish credibility and create curiosity quickly.

To Explore

- ☐ In preparation for your next performance review, ask yourself: (i) What have I accomplished? and (ii) Where do I want to go in the organization in the future?

- ☐ In preparation for a job interview, ask yourself: (i) What are my strengths? (ii) Which of my accomplishments are relevant to this role? (iii) What excites me about this position? and (iv) How will I establish a connection with my interviewer?

- ☐ If you love your current job/organization, ask yourself: How could I do more to let the company's leaders know how valuable I am?

- ☐ Where could I go to meet new people and share my story while doing something I enjoy?

Chapter Eight

Transforming Your Career

It is now time to apply all of these concepts and tools directly to your career. As I mentioned, I want to be known as practical. Practicality is a hallmark of my brand. Therefore, I would be remiss if I did not help you apply all of this information about self-promotion and all of these new storytelling skills to you and your career. After all, tools and skills are only good if you know how to use them effectively so that you reach your goals, right?

Goals, Targets and Actions

Think for a moment about your career goals. What would you like to accomplish in your career in the next twelve months? This may be an easy question for you to answer, either because you naturally set goals or because your organization has set some goals for you.

On the other hand, it may be a difficult question if you haven't given much thought to your goals recently. Goals are important and setting clear goals is a crucial first step in achieving anything. As Zig Ziglar said, "A goal properly set is halfway reached."[16]

Perhaps you know that you want to advance in your career but you do not know specifically what advancement looks like. Likely there is something you want to achieve or a change you want to make in your career. Consider what's currently working about your career and what's not working as well as you would like. Often our goals are buried within the answers to those questions.

Here are some other good questions to ponder:

- Do I want a promotion or a new role within my current company?
- Is there a particular project, case, division or team I want to be assigned to?
- Am I engaged in a job search or interested in looking for a new job?
- Would developing more business or bringing in new clients help me advance my career?

Clarifying your career goals is an important first step in the self-promotion process. Once you are clear about them, you can begin to determine how, where and when to self-promote. You can begin to identify the contexts and audiences for your self-promotion stories.

We can only successfully transform our careers if we strategically and effectively self-promote.

Who are the people with influence over whether you achieve the career goals you have identified? Think hard about this question. None of us can achieve our career goals without involving others. Our ability to achieve our goals depends upon getting noticed by the right people. We can only successfully transform our careers if we strategically and effectively self-promote.

If you want to be promoted, your boss and the leadership in your organization have to know you and your work. If you seek a new job, your prospective employer needs to know who you are, where your strengths lie and how you would fit within the organization. If you're developing business for yourself or your company, your prospects need to know who you are, what you do, how you do it and what makes you unique.

If you don't know the names of the people with influence over whether you achieve your career goals, that's okay. I bet you know what *types* of people they are — the hiring manager at X Co., the CEO of your key prospect or the person who was just tapped to lead the new project your company is undertaking.

It's important to identify the individuals by name and/or role who are in the best position to help you achieve your goals. These are the people who need to know you and hear your story. Put yourself in a position to tell your story to these people. They make up your target audience.

It's also important to consider what you need to do to get these influential people's attention. How do you get noticed by the people who can influence whether you achieve your goals? What are the actions you need to take to ensure that the key people you've identified know what they need to know to help you reach your goals? The more specific you can be about this, the better. Once you have identified the people and the action steps, you have put yourself in the driver's seat and can begin creating opportunities to interact with these key players.

Perhaps you need to tell your story more powerfully at your next performance review, and to do so, you need to begin to keep an accomplishment list. Maybe you need to work on the self-promotion story you tell when you're networking to ensure that you are establishing your credibility and creating curiosity within the first 20 seconds of any interaction. Perhaps you need to consider your strengths and the examples or mini-movies that best illustrate those strengths so you can shine in your next interview.

Or, maybe you need to prepare and practice so you are ready to capitalize on unexpected business opportunities that come your way on a plane, in the gym or at your child's school.

Clearly identifying your career goals and the members of your target audience will lead you to the specific self-promotion actions you need to take.

Accountability

Like my executive coaching clients, you will reach your career goals more quickly and easily if you have accountability. I suggest that you find a self-promotion partner — a buddy, a mentor or a coach — who can work with you as you seek to master the art of self-promotion. Let your self-promotion accountability partner know what your career goals are, who your target audience is and what you are going to do in order to share your story with those influential people. If you're having trouble with any of those three components, ask your accountability partner to help you brainstorm. Then, ask your partner to hold you accountable for taking the specific, concrete action steps you outline to grab the attention of your target audience so you can achieve your career goals. You can act as an accountability partner for that person as well.

Find out about his career goals, help him figure out who his target audience is, and what he needs to do to reach that audience. Ask him what he will do — "What specific actions will you take?" Also, ask him for a timeframe for taking those actions — "By when will you do that?" And, finally, make him accountable for letting you know what he has done — "How will I know what you have done?" Set up a regularly scheduled meeting or phone call with your accountability partner so you can both be held responsible for moving toward your career goals.

Your accountability partner can also help you gauge your self-promotion efforts. Remember that most of us are much less effective in our self-promotion efforts than we could be. Think back to the 0-10 scale I introduced in Chapter Four. Chances are you could increase the power of your self-promotion without coming close to being an over-promoter.

For you to reach the career goals you've identified, you will need to promote yourself at that higher level, and your self-promotion accountability partner can help you gauge that. Your partner can role play with you as you hone your self-promotion story for your target audience. She can give you feedback on your self-promotion efforts. She can tell you, on a scale of 0-10, where your self-promotion efforts are currently. Since we are the stars of our own stories, we are often unable to step back and hear them objectively.

Your self-promotion partner can also make suggestions about how you can increase the power and effectiveness of what you share and how you share it. She can point out how you can make your self-promotion story more engaging and suggest key details for you to share. She can tell you whether you've crossed the line and become an over-promoter, whether you need to amp up the power of your self-promotion efforts or whether you are operating within the most effective range.

As you work on mastering the art of self-promotion, I strongly urge you to ask someone to hold you accountable for preparing your stories, practicing them and ensuring that they hit the right tone for your target audience and context. You can't reach your career goals without other people, and you can't master the art of self-promotion without feedback. Make sure you get it!

To Know

- ❑ Clarifying your career goals is a critical step in the self-promotion process.
- ❑ Your ability to achieve your goals depends on your ability to promote yourself effectively and tell your story to the right people.
- ❑ Once you identify your career goals and the people who can help you achieve them, you can gain clarity on the specific self-promotion actions you need to take.
- ❑ With accountability, you're more likely to take the required actions and achieve the career goals you set out for yourself.

To Explore

- ❑ Set or revisit your career goals. Ask yourself: (i) What would I like to accomplish in my career in the next twelve months? (ii) Do I want a promotion or a new role within my current company? (iii) Is there a particular project, case, division or team I want to be assigned to? (iv) Do I want to find a new job? (v) Would developing more business or bringing in new clients help me advance my career?

- ❑ Who are the people that will have the most influence over whether I achieve my career goals?

- ❑ In service of my career goals, what specific actions do I need to take to ensure that those key people know my story?

- ❑ Find an accountability partner, share the principles from this book or ask them to read it. Then, ask for assistance in gauging your self-promotion efforts and following through on the actions you are committed to taking to reach your goals. You can provide your partner with accountability for reaching his goals too.

Chapter Nine

Putting It All Together

We've covered a lot of territory in these pages and you may feel a bit overwhelmed. I want you to resist the urge to get mired in that feeling and shift into action instead. Remember that you now have all of the tools and information you need to begin to master the art of self-promotion.

What should you do next? First, recognize that if, as a result of reading this book, you have begun to shift your mindset about self-promotion, you have already taken the critically important first step toward telling your story and transforming your career. If you have not yet shifted your mindset about self-promotion, then that is the best place to start. Dig deeply into your current mindset and work on creating a new, more empowering mindset that will enable you to move toward mastering the art of self-promotion.

Some Final Words

After you've taken that all-important first step, you can tap into the set of tools I have given you for telling your story. You can begin using those tools to move you toward your career goals. As you do so, I ask you to keep three key things in mind:

Number one — Be prepared. Be ready to self-promote at any time. Prepare and practice so that you can tell your story confidently in any context and to any audience. You never know when you may find yourself in an elevator with your company's CEO or sitting next to a prospective client on a plane.

Number two — Be yourself. Only you can effectively tell your story. Be authentic and sincere. Leverage your personality, your sense of humor and your passion. Allow your true self to shine through so people can connect and engage with you as you tell your story.

Number three — Be accountable. This book is only as good as what you implement. I want you to take action on what you've read here and take the time to engage in self-reflection. I want you to prepare your self-promotion stories thoroughly. I want you to ask someone to help you increase the power of your self-promotion efforts.

My company works with clients all over the country. We offer self-promotion coaching packages specifically designed to help you tell your story more effectively in light of your specific career goals and target audiences. And, if you don't know what your career goals are yet, we can help you discern those too. Whether you reach out to Novateur Partners for coaching, work with another coaching organization or simply find a self-promotion partner, be sure you get the accountability you need so you can reach your goals.

One more quick story as we close. My friend, Jane, recently told me about an interaction with her granddaughter, Brooke. Brooke is five years old and was showing Grandma Jane a drawing she made. Grandma Jane exclaimed over the drawing and told Brooke what a great artist she is. Brooke's response was classic. Brooke looked at Grandma Jane and said, "Thanks, Grandma. I am good at a lot of things and being an artist is just one of them." With the innocence of youth on her side, Brooke was able to recognize her own talents and speak freely about them without feeling self-conscious. She was able to promote herself comfortably and confidently. At the tender age of five, Brooke had mastered the art of self-promotion. And, isn't that what we all want to do?

Endnotes

1. Berlin, *Annie Get Your Gun.*
2. Sandberg, *Lean In.*
3. Collins, *Good to Great.*
4. www.freedictionary.com/mindset (accessed October 1, 2015).
5. Masters in Engineering Management Program, Pratt School of Engineering, Duke University.
6. Scott, *Fierce Conversations.*
7. Pink, *To Sell Is Human.*
8. Peters, "The Brand Called You." www.fastcompany.com/28905/brand-called-you (accessed October 1, 2015).
9. www.strengths.gallup.com/help/general/125540/strength.aspx (accessed October 1, 2015).
10. Rogers, "You Are Special."
11. Andy Stanley, Catalyst Dallas, August 9, 2011.
12. Godin, "define: Brand." http://sethgodin.typepad.com/seths_blog/2009/12/define-brand.html (accessed October 1, 2015).

13. McLaughlin, "What is a Brand, Anyway?" http://www.forbes.com/sites/jerrymclaughlin/2011/12/21/what-is-a-brand-anyway/ (accessed October 1, 2015).

14. McNally and Speak, *Be Your Own Brand.*

15. Peters, "The Brand Called You." www.fastcompany.com/28905/brand-called-you (accessed October 1, 2015).

16. Ziglar, "Official Ziglar Quotes." http://www.ziglar.com/quotes/zig-ziglar/goal-properly-set-halfway-reached (accessed October 8, 2015).

Acknowledgements

This project has taken over a year of my sustained time, energy and attention. It has also taken the combined efforts of an incredible group of people that I am fortunate enough to have surrounding me. My heartfelt gratitude goes out to:

My amazing clients who have taught me an infinite amount about the topic of self-promotion over the course of my coaching career and who are the source of the stories and examples in this book.

Bonnie Daneker whose knowledge, support and partnership have helped me take this book from a draft manuscript to a finished product.

Steven Sharp for his inspiration, encouragement and creativity.

Jennifer Bradley-Franklin for editing this book and sharing her writer's perspective with me.

Amena Ali, Andy Berg, Lisa Burke, Garrett D'Alessandro, Tom Flanigan, Jeff Haidet, Jennifer Kahnweiler, Emily

Kapit, Lori Patton, Kristy Weathers, Linda Wind and Alan Zimmerman for believing in me and this book.

La Tondra Murray and the Pratt Professional Masters Programs at Duke University for supporting my work in this arena year after year.

Duke University for inviting me to share this content with its alumni via webinar and live in Atlanta and Washington, DC. A special thank you to Bill Wright-Swadel and Teri Mills for championing this topic.

Rebecca Cummings for her friendship and for setting up our work zone days which created the accountability I needed to finish this book. Thank you also for pre-reading the book and providing valuable input.

Pam Freeman, Vicki Hudson, Paul Mendel and Steve Stone who volunteered to pre-read the manuscript and provided critical feedback.

Anne Yates who provided sound legal advice and counsel on intellectual property issues related to the book and helped this former IP attorney avoid becoming the cliché of the lawyer who represents herself.

Lori Ray, Novateur's Office Manager extraordinaire, without whom so much of this process would not have been possible.

The Novateur Partners team for being such a wonderful group of people to work and collaborate with every day.

Laurie Dugoniths and The Johnson Insurance Law Group for sharing their beautiful offices with Novateur and providing a great creative space.

All of the writers I have known and have been inspired by over the years including Myra McElhaney, Monica Parker, Greer Tirrill, and Christy Ziglar.

My coach, Helen House, for her powerful questions, deep listening and fierce championing throughout our work together.

Katie Schrier and the team at Barre3 South Buckhead who have helped me keep my mind and body fit throughout this process.

My longtime friend, Cathy Frazier, who has always believed in me and held me accountable and whose marketing mind has inspired me in all things self-promotion.

My parents, Mike and Luise Stone, my son, Matt Grossman, and my whole family for always supporting me and loving me.

My amazing husband, Dan Sheedy, who has shown me unconditional love day in and day out while I have worked on this project and whose positivity, humor and determination are a daily inspiration.

I have learned a great deal through this creative process and want to thank you all for your contributions, your wisdom and your support.

About the Author

Photo by Erik Meadows

Debby Stone, JD, CPCC, PCC is the founder of Novateur Partners, an executive coaching and leadership development consultancy serving corporate leaders, entrepreneurs, lawyers and the organizations in which they work. Novateur is known for combining extensive real-world experience with entrepreneurial creativity to assist its clients in developing practical strategies for success.

As a professional speaker, Debby has presented programs at corporations, law firms, professional associations, educational conferences and universities. She leverages her breadth of experience to connect with audiences in various industries including finance, law, engineering, government, real estate, travel, entertainment and technology.

Prior to embarking on her coaching and speaking career, Debby practiced law for 16 years and worked as a management consultant at Bain & Company.

(over)

Debby graduated *magna cum laude* from Duke University's Sanford School of Public Policy and a holds a JD with High Honors from the Duke University School of Law. She received her certification as a professional co-active coach through the Coaches Training Institute and has earned the credential of Professional Certified Coach from the International Coach Federation.

Debby has been quoted in numerous publications including *The Wall Street Journal* and has been featured in several books including *45 is the New 25* and *Good Enough is the New Perfect.*

When she is not coaching or speaking, Debby contributes her time to several non-profit organizations. She is a foodie who enjoys running, reading and traveling. She is also an avid Duke basketball fan. Although Debby's work knows no geographic boundaries, she and her husband live in Atlanta.

If you would like to book Debby Stone to speak at a conference, sales kick-off, corporate retreat, lunch and learn or other event, please contact her via Novateur Partners – info@novateurpartners.com and 404-975-3000.

About Novateur Partners

Novateur Partners is an executive coaching and leadership development consultancy. Novateur Partners offers:

- Individual Coaching
- Group/Team Coaching
- Strategic Planning
- Retreat Facilitation
- Public Speaking Training/Coaching
- Workshops
- Assessments

Self-Promotion coaching packages are available. For more information please visit www.artofselfpromotionbook.com.

Please email info@novateurpartners.com for information on bulk discounts on book purchases or for more information about our services.